"John Wilkinson stands traditional ap
ing new vision of conversational eng
wonder and the apparent 'absurdity' of faith, Wilkinson in one move
makes way for an altogether different kind of engagement for those who
would consider the spiritual journey Christ invites us into. With an
equal poetic power, *No Argument for God* provides a breathtaking visage
of another world waiting for those who would embrace the mystery of
knowing God both here and in the world to come. Not just another
voice in the current debate of what apologetics should look like in a
postmodern milieu, Wilkinson's fresh approach changes the very nature
of the conversation itself. To think that wonder, mystery and the obvious transcendence of faith from mere reason may be the actual strengths
of our historic faith instead of the ugly stepchildren they've historically
been is freeing and sets a new course for both evangelism and our personal relationship with God himself."

R. York Moore, national evangelist, InterVarsity Christian Fellowship/USA

"John Wilkinson's book represents one of the best responses to the attacks of modernist 'scholars' who insist that their limited view of the
world is all that there could possibly be. I especially appreciate that John
has at the core presented that our response should be focused on the
absurdity of the gospel, not only today but even in the first century. He
reminds us that faith is rooted not in our ability to reach beyond the sky
and 'understand' God or even 'discover' the Creator, but in our Lord's
desire to reach through time and space and live among us. The continually fresh and foolishly profound purity of the stand-alone Deity caring
enough to invite us—any of us, each of us—into his reign as King of all
things, seen and unseen, is what makes faith the wonder of all wonders.
Well done, John Wilkinson, keeping us on track as little children set
free by the voice and embrace of the One who has come and beckoned,
"Let the little children come to me . . .'"

Chap Clark, professor of youth, family and culture,
Fuller Theological Seminary

JOHN WILKINSON

NO ARGUMENT FOR GOD

GOING BEYOND REASON IN
CONVERSATIONS ABOUT FAITH

IVP Books

An imprint of InterVarsity Press
Downers Grove, Illinois

InterVarsity Press
P.O. Box 1400, Downers Grove, IL 60515-1426
World Wide Web: www.ivpress.com
Email: email@ivpress.com

InterVarsity Press® is the book-publishing division of InterVarsity Christian Fellowship/USA®, a movement of students and faculty active on campus at hundreds of universities, colleges and schools of nursing in the United States of America, and a member movement of the International Fellowship of Evangelical Students. For information about local and regional activities, write Public Relations Dept., InterVarsity Christian Fellowship/USA, 6400 Schroeder Rd., P.O. Box 7895, Madison, WI 53707-7895, or visit the IVCF website at <www.intervarsity.org>.

Design: Cindy Kiple

Images: Bodhi Hill/iStockphoto

ISBN 978-0-8308-3420-4

Printed in Canada ∞

InterVarsity Press is committed to protecting the environment and to the responsible use of natural resources. As a member of Green Press Initiative we use recycled paper whenever possible. To learn more about the Green Press Initiative, visit <www.greenpressinitiative.org>.

Library of Congress Cataloging-in-Publication Data

Wilkinson, John
   No argument for God: going beyond reason in conversations about
faith/John Wilkinson.
     p. cm.
   Includes bibliographical references.
   ISBN 978-0-8308-3420-4 (pbk.: alk. paper)
   1. Faith and reason—Christianity. 2. Apologetics. I. Title.
   BT50.W4725 2010
   231'.042—dc22

                                            2010040600

P	17	16	15	14	13	12	11	10	9	8	7	6	5	4	3	2	1
Y	25	24	23	22	21	20	19	18	17	16	15	14	13	12	11		

*This book is for everyone who has ever been
labeled "different." Enjoy the gift.*

CONTENTS

There are more things in heaven and earth, Horatio,

Than are dreamt of in your philosophy.

HAMLET, ACT 1, SCENE 5

1

WOULDN'T IT BE NICE?

AN OLD FRIEND WHO I HADN'T SEEN SINCE high school recently
popped up on Facebook. I smiled as I saw his photos and noticed
a little less hair and a little more weight, but his quirky smile was
still the same. As I read his information profile, I remembered
how cynical he could be. In describing his political affiliation, he
wrote, "Nothing changes anyway . . ." I laughed. Then I read his
entry under *religious views:* "Wouldn't that be nice?"

Now I am no expert on Facebook entries. I understand that
Mike was probably just trying to breeze through a bunch of profile questions with a touch of wit, but this caption caught me off
guard. I pondered that question for a little while. What an interesting question.

Of course the question is really no question at all; it is nothing
more than a curt way to express his skepticism. What he means
is, It's a shame faith isn't real. If I could guess at what he was
thinking, he would probably say that Santa Claus, the Easter
Bunny, the Tooth Fairy and Tinkerbell are all nice ideas, but
they are only that—ideas, feelings, sentiments. So, for my friend,
God falls into this category as well. Wouldn't it be nice if it were

all true? The question is actually a statement. Faith is a nice idea, for the delusional.

If he had entered "Atheist" or "I don't have any religious beliefs," I don't think I would have taken as much notice. There is something about "Wouldn't it be nice?" that annoyed me. There is something so defeatist about it. Just because it is a beautiful idea does not make it a fairy tale. As if to say that having one ultimate source of knowledge and purpose that is just too good to be true is what makes it ultimately false. Wouldn't it be nice if all of this we see around us had purpose, that this crazy world is not adrift in meaninglessness, and that at the end of the day there is Someone who stays awake and looks over us, cares for us and loves us.

It would be nice, actually.

It would be nice if we weren't alone on this small planet in the midst of seemingly infinite blackness, because as humans we long for relationship. It would be nice if someone had a plan for our lives, because living merely for ourselves is an empty pursuit. It would be nice to know someone is rooting for us, someone who knew us in the most intimate way and still approved. It would be nice to have someone we could ask for help, confidence, mercy, grace. It would be nice to have the help and guidance of someone beyond our finite humanity, because there are some things that we just can't accomplish on our own.

I am increasingly troubled by the growing distrust of the very things we would love to see. It is tragic that people could potentially miss out on something as rich as a relationship with their Creator or the warmth of forgiveness and acceptance of their God just because it seems too good to be true. Isn't it strange that just because something happens to agree with our deepest longings, we assume it can't be real? Wouldn't the opposite be just as true: Since there is a worldwide ancient desire for something Other, there must be something to it?

Now traditionally Christians have taken issue with the likes of my friend and developed impressive arguments to prove their faith. These arguments are used to debate skeptics and somehow convince them that faith has a rational foundation. Though research has uncovered some interesting facts about the reliability of the Bible and the historical record of Christianity, these debates rarely do anything more than solidify the positions of either side. To be honest, I don't think we even need to engage in a debate. What if there were no argument for God?

Imagine agreeing with the "Wouldn't it be nice" people: You are right, there are a lot of elements of Christianity that just seem absurd.

But is there room for conversation after saying this?

I don't mean to say Christian faith is untrue. Let's face it, if there is no God—that is, there is no purpose to anything and religion is a fairy tale—would we have discovered it? Is it possible to discover something that doesn't exist? C. S. Lewis put it succinctly, "If the whole universe has no meaning, we should never have found out that it has no meaning."[1] So I am not encouraging us to side with atheists and give up on faith. Faith has had traction with humanity for millennia and with great purpose. No, I am not saying that faith is untrue, just unreasonable.

Perhaps it is not so much *un*-reasonable as it is *beyond* reasonable. No doubt you have heard the sometimes overused analogy of ants. In this analogy, imagine you have an ant farm and have become so delighted with the ants that you want to communicate with them. Repeated attempts to talk to them through the glass gets you nowhere; they just keep tunneling through dirt doing their ant thing. You try tapping on the glass. No good; imagine a huge finger from the sky about three miles wide apparently smashing the atmosphere on a cloudless day. Ant panic.

Now assume you are able to talk with one of them using some

sort of translator device. Even then, everything you say would be
ridiculous. Imagine trying to share your life with an ant. Your
daily life of cars, iPods and blenders would be nonsense to an ant.
Everything would have to be mediated by some sort of story or
symbol that would help the ant grasp what you are talking about.
In a world of *find food, build dwelling, make more ants*, how would an
ant grasp your favorite song or your typical day?

In the same way, when we talk about things (like God) that are
outside the experience of our current existence, we can say that
they are (in the most literal way) *nonsense*, that is, beyond the domain of the senses. So when we talk about the possibility of God
and what that means for us, we have to take absurdity and nonsense as starting points. We must do so especially as we speak of
the Christian faith, because God decided to reveal himself to us
through the person of Jesus. If we take seriously that Jesus was
from a completely different existence, the things that he spoke of
were beyond our world of five senses. As such they break traditional rules of logic; in fact, they must in order to be authentic.
There truly is no argument for God that is capable of bearing the
weight of his existence. Things that operate within the realm of
human reason bear the fingerprints of human inventors. The stuff
of God, however, doesn't just sound strange, it *is* strange.

Let's pause here for a second. Chances are you have never
been encouraged by someone who believes in God to see that
faith is absurd. I have had several friends who wanted me to see
faith as nonsense and give it up. I have resisted them and usually
tried to give reasons for belief. Indeed, Christianity does have
logically convincing ideas that can lead someone to belief, and
we'll discuss some of these toward the end of the book. More
recently, however, I have wondered why one has to necessarily
lead to the other. Why does the fact that faith is hard to accept
logically become the end of the argument rather than the be-

ginning of something different? In fact, maybe the more we let go of our secure grip on what makes sense, the more vibrant our faith will become.

■ ■ ■

Think for just a moment how absurd faith really is.

The Bible opens with God—a superhuman, fatherly type who at some point before time spoke everything into existence. With no tools, no material, no floor, no ceiling, from somewhere beyond everything we know, he simply said "Let there be" and it was so. This is hard to even imagine. How does someone create with no materials? Where was God standing when there was nothing? The Bible says that God was hovering over the surface of the waters as he spoke things into existence. What water? Do we take literally that God has wings? Or a mouth to speak with? Even if we take it figuratively, where did God come from when he decided to create?

The centerpiece of Christian theology states that God became human in the person of Jesus. Listen to how crazy that sounds: God had a Son who came to earth as a human. He was completely God *and* completely human at the same time. This means he could get hungry and tired, but also walk on water. Though he was beaten, he could raise people from the dead. As if this isn't confusing enough, God died on a cross. Read it again—*God died!* Christian theologians have wrestled with the meaning of this idea for centuries, and we are still no closer to full comprehension than when we first began.

Now imagine how illogical the Christian idea of atonement is: *God sent himself to pay himself for the sins against himself.*

How does that add up? I have sinned against God and by so doing deserve eternal separation from God, but Jesus' death paid the price of my sin so that God and I can be eternally reconciled.

But if God is God, and Jesus is God, and I am me, how does God
pay God for my sin? Isn't that like God taking a hundred dollar bill
from his left pocket to put it in his right pocket? If I borrow your
car and get in a wreck, it is one thing for you to forgive me. It is
quite another for you to write me a check so that I can hand the
check back to you so that we are even. It doesn't seem to add up!

Think about what happens when you die. If you are a believer,
then you believe that you will one day rise from the dead. Though
your body has decomposed and turned to dust, you will live again.
We are not exactly sure how it works. Does the soul leave the
body at death and go to heaven? Does God reanimate and recon-
stitute the body sometime in the future? Well, these things sound
nice, but not everyone agrees on how it happens. Again, theologians have had fun picking these things apart for centuries. The
only thing we know for sure is that upon death bodies slowly turn
back to dust.

So it is easy to see how someone can arrive at the conclusion
that it all seems a bit irrational. On the one hand, there is what we
know for sure (people die and turn to dust), and on the other is
the belief that we will live again someday (wouldn't it be nice).
Most believers, without realizing it, absorb what our parents,
Sunday school teachers or culture have taught us about faith, and
we've made it our own with very little critical reflection. You
don't think this has happened to you? Try answering some of
these questions without an "um, . . ." "I think I read . . ." or
"Wasn't there that movie about . . . ?"

- What is a soul? Where is it?
- Where is heaven?
- What is an angel?
- When we get to heaven, will we have memories of life here on
  earth? What about bad memories?

Think about how difficult these questions are. Now look at how absurd some of our answers are—full of uncertainty and conjecture.

Now let's look at what the Bible says about the future. Not only does the Christian faith say that we will be raised from the dead, but the whole universe will be renovated when Jesus returns. According to the Bible, Jesus will return to earth in order to renew the dwelling place of humans and make it a dwelling place with God. The Bible speaks of God creating a *new* heaven and a *new* earth. Everything gets cleaned, renewed and perfected: greenhouse gases, carbon footprints, clear-cut forests and smokestack particulates— all gone. It vanishes in one moment on the Last Day as God presents us with a city to live in. Time begins with a garden and then ends with a city. The book of Revelation puts it this way:

> I heard a loud voice from the throne saying, "Now the dwelling of God is with men, and he will live with them. They will be his people, and God himself will be with them and be their God. He will wipe every tear from their eyes. There will be no more death or mourning or crying or pain, for the old order of things has passed away." (Revelation 21:3-4)

It all sounds so wonderful, so beautiful . . . *wouldn't it be nice?*

Yes, it would be nice, but the fact that faith is so warm and fuzzy only reveals how far from reality it is. Faith is nice, and nice isn't real. Real is what we can see and test and verify. Real is here and now and observable. We can learn what is real from what we see and sense, because it is tied to logic. For example, in school we learned the law of the conservation of matter, that matter cannot be created or destroyed. As a result, the Bible's account of creation reads like a storybook compared to the hard science of "what we know." Simple logic tells us something cannot be items A and B at the same time. Applying this to Christianity, the "fully God, fully human" thing begins to look ridiculous. When the goal of our development is critical thinking, fact trumps faith and the "real" takes precedence over what lies beyond the senses. A false dichotomy is set up between the "real" and the "not real," and science is set up as certainty while faith is presented as nonsense.

This is an important distinction, because when I say faith is nonsense I don't mean that it is not real. I mean quite literally "not of the senses," something that exceeds the grasp of human sense organs and the reason that is fashioned from them. Simply put, sense and reason are only one slim pathway of what can be known. Just because faith doesn't reside completely in this pathway doesn't make it a fairy tale. It's crazy to think that all that can be known, can be known by humans. Yes, the scope of human knowledge is vast, but we quickly forget that it belongs to a small subset of total knowledge. There are paths that stretch far beyond the human ability to understand.

What do those paths of thinking look like? For me, as an inquisitive kid, I started to wonder why we are here. I tried to read the Bible but got stuck in Genesis. I tried asking my priest questions, but he was pretty evasive. I remember one Sunday standing at the back door of the church after services. He had preached on something I had questions about. After asking him a few questions about the Bible while standing in the doorway of our church, the organist peered over the priest's shoulder and huffed that I might be taking the Bible too literally. My priest agreed. I made a mental note that day: beware of organists with the last name of Stanke. That woman was scary. More importantly, I was beginning to understand that the Bible was not as simple as I thought. I was confused and didn't know where to turn. One day I saw a TV commercial that depicted a man walking on a beach, with a voice-over asking questions like, *Why am I here? What is the purpose of life? Are there answers?* The funny thing is that this commercial was aimed at forty-somethings—upwardly mobile professionals—and there I was at twelve, eyes glued to the TV thinking, *Good questions!*

So I called the number on the screen and asked for my free book called *Power for Living*. The fact that it was free was the clincher—I *had* to have this book. When I got my hands on it, I devoured it. It was a series of biographies of professionals and sports celebrities who had trusted their lives to Jesus. In the back of the book was an outline for how to put my trust in Christ. This is where I froze—I was unsure of what it meant to have someone "come into your heart." I feared the idea of someone actually coming into my body, into my heart. The idea of a strange force invading my body and making me do things that *it* wanted to do upset me. I wanted to call the shots.

The whole thing was ridiculous. There I was stopping short of attaining eternal salvation because I was afraid that if Jesus didn't like Froot Loops I wouldn't be able to eat them. (Our family didn't even have Froot Loops in the house, so I was definitely overthinking this.) The feeling was real, though—like I was on a high dive with everyone watching. What should I do? What if I jump, and the result is the opposite of what I expected? I wanted to live *my* life, not have someone else's life lived through me. I had heard other people talk about Jesus and always considered them to be freaks. How could someone bleeding two thousand years ago do anything for me today? Does any of this make sense?

To make a long story short, I jumped. I did what was unreasonable and illogical. I trusted in someone I couldn't see, hear, taste or feel. I did the absurd. It wouldn't be the last time.

I spent the next six weeks trying to convince my parents I didn't join a cult. There is something unnerving to parents about having a child proclaim that he is born again. It didn't help in the weeks to come when I had a theological discussion with my parents and affirmed that they were going to hell if they didn't do

what I had done. Twelve-year-olds are annoying enough without
the "you are going to hell" speech. Christ had come into my life,
but I still had the tact of a tween. Though I was clumsy and awkward in expression, I felt like I had latched onto something great
and unexplainable. I wanted them to *feel* what I had done, but
explaining it was difficult.

I eventually went to Penn State University, where I studied philosophy and religion. Between twelve and eighteen I had read several books on Christianity and listened to kooky pastors on the
radio. I was ready to talk about my faith with my professors. I figured one or two would give their lives to Christ. Really. Then I
met Dr. Peterson. He was a plucky professor with a bald head, large
glasses, quick wit and smile. He looked harmless, but looks are de-
ceiving in academia, and each day brought another assault on my
faith. Dr. Peterson, it seemed, saw as his mission to suck the faith
out of every student. He would get into long and intense arguments
with students as an attempt to expose the absurdity of faith. There
were stories of people who had left the faith because of Dr. Peterson. He was a legendary spiritual Goliath.

It's hard debating someone who can run circles around you
intellectually. I reached a point where I felt tapped out. I had spent
the last half dozen years reading books and listening to others
about the Christian faith, and generally developing *reasons* for my
belief. I thought I had become a good apologist, but I was faring
miserably at the hands of my first real challenge. This was frustrating—I had already nailed down faith. I had made the most
important discovery, eternal life, and made sense of Jesus. These
were settled issues. At this point I felt I should be building on
these foundations instead of questioning them.

I was miserable. I wasn't sure what to believe. One night I went
back to my room, didn't turn on the lights, locked the door, knelt
by my bed and started to cry. I was scared, tired and confused. I

was supposed to have a lot more answers. I had become a huge disappointment. All my reasons for believing were being dismantled. My mind went blank and something escaped my lips— "Lord, I have no reason to believe in you."

Admitting this felt traitorous. I couldn't believe that I said it! This faith, which ignited within me six years prior, now looked like it was becoming doused by reason. At that moment I faced two paths. To the right I could embrace my faith but had to let go of my intellect. I would retain my relationship with God but lose what I had come to learn. I would be stupid—but full of faith. To the left I could embrace reason and logic, and let go of my faith. I would learn the things my professor knew and walk the path he walked, saying goodbye to my journey of faith.

A deep dread overwhelmed me. It was dark and felt as if someone were standing on my chest. These were very big things to begin considering. You can have this kind of back and forth about someone you are dating or whether you will take this job or that, but facing this kind of fork in the road about faith is much more weighty. Like weighing the pros and cons of a divorce, even the thought of it makes you sick. Had I simply come to the end of a phase? Then again, what if this was the biggest test of my faith? My life as I knew it, both here and eternal, hung in the balance.

And so I was confronted with fear at a pivotal point in my life. Once again, I was up on the high dive. That night in my room I was scared about what lay ahead. I was worried that a part of me was dying—that my faith journey was coming to an end. But even more, I was afraid of how I would have to change if I wanted to keep my faith. I did not like the idea of not taking the intellectual side of me seriously. To continue in this faith, I felt that I had to abandon my intellect. On the other hand, a life of rejecting God felt lonely, cold and soulless, but a life of stupidity felt hollow, fake and untrue. Everything I knew, all my reasons for believing—

the fulfilled prophecies, the archaeology that supported the Bible, all the facts that I had accumulated—fell apart upon meeting Dr. Peterson. The good reasons for belief had become mere reason, an intellectual Ping-Pong match between those who choose to believe and those who don't. I was frozen in fear because I *wanted* to believe but wasn't sure that I could. I imagined it would have been better to have remained ignorant. But that was not a choice for me now.

So I had an important decision to make—do I jump or go back down the ladder? To go back down the ladder is respectable. I leave with something intact. If I leave this all behind, at least I retain my intellect. I can go on living and learning and not have to worry about the life of faith. Reason wins. Conversely, if I jump off the high dive, I have my faith in God. Even though I would have no intellectual credibility, I could claim to be a person who believes. Both were choices that would leave me with less. One thing was certain to me that night. If I was going to choose faith, I would have to let go and jump in. I couldn't stand on the board and experience the dive. In order to feel faith, I needed to have faith. In order for it all to make sense, I had to abandon sense.

And I did. At a certain point I prayed, "God, I *choose* to believe in you, even though I have no reason to." The answer was a long time coming, but so very simple. Instead of it becoming an end of an intellectual journey, it became the beginning. What does faith look like when it is larger than human reason? Who does God become after the arguments?

It was shortly after I leaped that I felt a very calming and soothing presence. Something like a warm hand on my shoulders. I heard, "There, now we can begin." I felt that God had removed the core of what I thought was faith and replaced it with my decision to believe *in spite of the reasons not to.* Believing because I *choose* to believe is a lot different than believing because of the overwhelming evidence of the resurrection of Christ. Instead of intellectual arguments being the core of my faith, my decision to believe in the extraordinary work and person of Christ became the core of moving forward in my faith. There was still a place for the intellect, but it would have to be layered over the core of a decision.

I had no idea what a huge step I had made that day. I thought I was cutting off a side of me that hinders faith. In fact, I had stepped outside of a restrictive view of what truth really is. To think that the truth about anything can fit within our small frame of reference is nothing short of arrogance. That day I took another step in my journey, which started with the absurd rather than trying to deny it.

So when one of my atheist friends tells me that faith is irrational, I agree and then ask my friend to walk with me down a path beyond reason, logic and sense to see if by abandoning our arguments for God we can find him. So when I invite you to look at faith as nonsense, please understand that I take Scripture, experience and reason very seriously, just in their proper order. And as a courtesy to my high school friend, let's look at the absurdity of faith first.

2

SEEING THINGS

FOR THE FIRST TIME

EVERYONE NEEDS TO TAKE A TRIP to a foreign culture. We learn a lot by seeing things for the first time. One of the longest trips I have ever taken was to the Philippine Islands. Besides being a trip to the other side of the world (and twenty-two hours in a plane), it was an adventure of new experiences. When we arrived, I stepped out of the airport and into a heat unlike anything I had previously felt. It wasn't just hot; it was like stepping into a boiler room. I thought my face would melt. It was so humid I could *see* the air. I stepped off the curb and shook hands with my friend; at first I thought he had a hand-sweating problem. As I met more people that day I realized that *everyone* in the Philippines has a hand-sweating problem. When it is 95 degrees with 150 percent humidity, sweat is a way of life.

We packed ourselves into a small car and drove through the city. I don't know how we survived. I gripped the side of my seat as we were catapulted down streets with no apparent traffic laws. (My Filipino friends chatted happily.) To me, the city of Manila was complete chaos. There were people everywhere—walking; on bikes; in cars, buses and jeepneys; and pushing carts and wagons. All of them were going somewhere—fast.

Personal space is conceived of differently in the Philippines than in the United States. Four or five people per taxi was normal. When we loaded our group into the back of a truck, we sat so close together we were sharing organs. The highlight of that first day was watching a moped pass us with a sidecar carrying thirteen people. Yes, thirteen! Can you imagine that many people smashed together on a moped going about thirty-five miles per hour? I had never seen such sights. To my friend, what was a typical day in the city felt like complete craziness to me.

When we arrived where we were staying, my experience was no different. Conflicting odors of chicken and beef cooked by street vendors mingled with diesel in the heavy, humid air. One smell I will never forget is ballut. Ballut, a Filipino delicacy, is essentially the egg of a fertilized chick or duck two weeks shy of hatching. Yum. Boiled on the street, ballut is eaten by cracking the egg, drinking the amniotic juice and eating the little boiled chick, feathers and all. My friends laughed at my gag reflex. It was a real treat for them; for me it was an animal-rights issue.

While I never truly adjusted to the idea of ballut, I did become acclimated to the Filipino way of life. I adjusted to the heat and the smell of diesel, and I even developed a hand-sweating problem. I changed from a nervous visitor to a participant in the culture. I learned to relax in taxis as they ricocheted through town. Though I stayed for less than a month, the masses seemed less chaotic and more inviting. In a strange way, thirteen men on a moped began to make sense to me. The foreign had become familiar. I began to lose sight of the way things appeared to me as a visitor. This is what happens to us; the familiar can sometimes blind us to what is right under our nose. Seeing what we have grown up with is like smelling our own breath. The things that are closest to us are the least noticeable.

The same is true when we look at our beliefs. Some may have a tough time viewing faith as nonsense, but the familiarity of our faith may blind us to its obvious absurdities. When we hear that faith is nonsense, it is natural to take exception or at least to be offended, but try looking at faith as if you are seeing it for the first time, like a tourist. To save the world a man builds a big boat in the desert. Angels talk to humans. God's Son returns on clouds. Is it possible that these have become so familiar to us that their absurdity is no longer evident? But our resistance is understandable. Questioning our faith seems to ridicule the world we have established our lives on, one that was formed by people we love and respect.

Recounting the absurdities of our faith forces us to realize that in its purest form Christianity does not conform to human logic. Over the centuries these absurd details could have been edited and cleaned up to fit within the bounds of reason, but they haven't. Only in the last few hundred years have the faithful felt compelled to *make sense* of Christianity. So we resist acknowledging the nonsense of Christianity. If we agree that Christianity doesn't make sense, we fear it will lose validity—revealing that Christianity is wrong. But what I hope to investigate in this book is that perhaps the absurdity of faith is the only way to validate it conclusively. If we are looking for something that proves our faith, logic or reason won't do it. Ironically, it is the fact that our faith is so strange that makes it so logically compelling.

So let's look at Christianity with the same objectivity we would use to understand Haitian voodoo. Let's try to imagine what Christianity would look like if we had never been to church, never read the Bible or prayed. Imagine the difficulty of understanding ideas like grace (love your enemies) or the atonement (God handed his Son over to die for us). As we step into this sometimes uncomfortable exercise, remember that the more it seems contrary to reason, the more it bears the imprint of something wholly Other.

At our first tourist stop we will visit a church and examine Christian practices. The church and its worship are very strange phenomena. Where else do people (some of them complete strangers to one another) sing songs, read stories from an ancient book and listen to a speech on how to live? Some churches feature robes and rituals; others, T-shirts and a rock show. Most churches feature a cross—a symbol of an ancient execution. Strange. Bread (or wafers) and wine (or grape juice) are distributed as the *body* and *blood* of a someone who died over two thousand years ago. The songs, rituals and symbols on a Sunday morning all refer to events thousands of years in the past. The point of the morning is to worship someone or something unseen and unheard by most. At the end of the time together, someone passes a plate or a basket to collect money. If this were your first time seeing all of this, it may look to you like an elaborate scam.

If this were a different religion, say Hinduism, wouldn't you find it odd that they believe in something or someone that very few will ever admit to seeing or hearing? It would be hard to understand how the actions of an ancient religious figure can influence the present. Would the religious rituals seem a bit gory? Wouldn't these make God sound violent? And what about worship? Doesn't that make God sound narcissistic? How about the collection plate? Who gets the money? We'll listen to someone tell us what to believe or how to behave from a book thousands of years old and then he or she asks us for money. Shouldn't the speaker be paying *us*?

Perhaps the strangest thing is that, for all the effort, Christians are no different than anyone else. Groups of people get together once a week, hold hands and sing to an invisible deity. When it is

over they go back to a life that is just like everyone else's—same
number of divorces, same number of cheaters, liars, pedophiles,
sin and humanity. This is perhaps the greatest irrational element:
groups of people who study a holy book act just like everyone
else. It doesn't make any sense. Whether their worship is high
liturgy or more like a rock concert, millions of people on Sunday
mornings bow their heads, close their eyes and talk to Someone
that no one has ever seen and only a slim minority claim to have
heard, and they aren't any different because of it. Strange!

As a tourist, prayer would strike me as the strangest activity.
Let's say that we know a Mrs. Jones, who is having back surgery to
alleviate pain. She has asked members of the church to pray that
the surgery goes well. Now, praying for Mrs. Jones's surgery is a
nice gesture, but what is really taking place? Is she being healed or
operated on? Does God work through scalpels? If they pray for her
to be healed, why take her to a surgeon? As a tourist, I would think
that if prayer works, they should skip surgery and stick with praying. Otherwise, it seems they have hedged their bet.

If they pray for healing and it doesn't happen, is it their fault?
Not enough prayer? Not for the right thing? Is it God's fault?
Doesn't he want to answer their prayer? Even if God answers this
prayer, there are countless other prayers that are either unanswered
or answered negatively. But if God is good, why would prayers for
healing be rejected? A group of skeptics was so affected by this
question they started an organization asking, "Why does God
hate amputees?" They make the very sharp point that no amount
of prayer has restored an amputee. God's silence to such prayers of
healing interferes with our clean and neat theologies on prayer.

If the weekly religious behavior of Christians strains logic, it is
fed by a theology that is even more burdensome. The Old Testament showcases an ancient tribal family's involvement with God,
who helps them survive in the midst of the Assyrian, Persian and

Egyptian superpowers. Why didn't God choose the Ming dynasty? The Mayans? The Greeks? God ignores these more advanced peoples and picks Abraham's descendants, Israel, slaves in Egypt. If the goal is to reach a universal audience, this is an odd choice.

The climax of God's involvement with this group produces a very violent emancipation. In an apparent showdown with the gods of Egypt, Israel's God delivers a series of plagues on the Egyptians. Livestock are slaughtered, rivers turn to blood, and firstborn sons are killed. Apparently God is not to be trifled with. Having kicked in the door of Egypt, God leads his people into the desert to covenant with them on Mount Sinai. This covenant is an intimate process in which God reveals himself to his people through delivering his law.

The Old Testament law is pretty remarkable. Most people are familiar with the Ten Commandments, but these are just a small section of laws that fill the first five books of the Bible. A detailed reading of these laws reveals a unique genius. Not just content with prohibiting certain actions, the Old Testament law addresses personal intent. For example, coveting our neighbor's wife (or presumably our neighbor's husband) is prohibited. Imagine how different our world would be if we took seriously something like coveting. And then there's the law that commands people to help their neighbor's donkey get back home, and even one that commands us to help our *enemy's* donkey! The law is focused on the *whole* person—not just a piece of us. The Israelites were to love God with all their heart, mind and soul. The law sought to transform a person from the inside out.

Mixed among these laws, however, are some laws that are either confusing or objectionable (or both!). What's with a law that prohibits wearing clothing with mixed fibers? Now, to be fair, there are a handful of social and historical observations that help us understand the context and culture of many passages, but some remain difficult. Take, for example, the law that mandates capital punishment for a disobedient child. Knowing the culture can help, but ultimately we struggle with the Old Testament as we see Yahweh encouraging war, animal sacrifice and slaying children. These real head scratchers give us pause; we wonder why they're there.

The New Testament is even more bizarre. Remember, as tourists who know no Christian theology, imagine how nonsensical the incarnation would be. This is a big one—God, previously accepted as one being, has a Son (and, we find later, a Holy Spirit). The God of the universe has a Son? What does that mean? Is he equal with or subordinate to God? The eternal Son takes on flesh, becoming the human Jesus of Nazareth, who is still God but is also fully human. Though he emptied himself of God's glory, he had the power to raise people from the dead. In one of the most famous encounters in the Bible, God's Son is tempted by Satan. Can someone unable to sin—God—be tempted? He must have had the *choice*. If Jesus had the choice, then he had the ability. How does God have an ability to sin? All this is hard to understand, and at times it seems to be completely paradoxical.

These are just a few samples of Christian belief that are difficult to line up with reason. Some have responded by sidestepping these dirty details of the Bible's stories for the ethics of Christianity. Since the Bible stories and laws are hard to square with reason, we can safely embrace the more sensible ethics of the Bible: *love your neighbor, turn the other cheek,* and *do unto others as you would have them do unto you.* Regardless of the theological fine print, you can't argue with the supremacy of Christian ethics, right?

Perhaps, but then we begin to look at the specific commands of Jesus in the Sermon on the Mount. Arguably the crown jewel of the Gospels, the Sermon on the Mount has some interesting implications for the believer. I've already mentioned turning the other cheek, but what is this really asking of us? Essentially, Jesus is saying that when an enemy backhands us on one cheek, we should turn and offer the offender the other cheek for another hit. Just from a human dignity standpoint, it doesn't seem to make sense to submit to the humiliation of another. Certainly Jesus can see that by offering the other cheek the victim only perpetuates a cycle of violence! Do abusers learn by grace, or do they trample it?

In the same sermon Jesus continues by saying that if someone forces us to walk a mile, go two, and if someone sues us for our coat, we should give the person our shirt as well. It is commonly accepted that Jesus was referring to Roman soldiers, who were legally empowered to force Jews to carry their gear up to a mile, or hand over their coats. So Christ's ethic goes beyond obeying oppressive rule; we should double the demand. These same Roman soldiers were known for their savagery. The Jews hated Rome in part because when going to or returning from battle the Roman soldiers raped the women and plundered the towns they passed. If reason were our guide, Jesus' suggestion that ancient Jews go beyond the requirement of the Roman law is either remarkably naive or ignorant.

Since Christian ethics have an eye on the next life, the slant will always be in favor of the oppressor. With heaven in the equation, what does it matter if people here misuse and abuse us? This serves both the oppressor and the oppressed. Christian martyrs get their reward in heaven, and tyrants get submissive masses. Christian submission is a dictator's dream because it gives incentive for the oppressed to remain subordinate. So we should accept the backhands of evil people, but we should not misuse God's name? We should carry the shields and swords of monsters an extra mile, but not have sex before marriage? These ethics don't seem to fit within reason.

Regardless of the theological fine print, who can argue with all the good Christians have done for the poor and the needy in the name of Christ? Hospitals, orphanages, adoption services, and charities for the poor and underprivileged are the direct result of the Christian mission in the world. This is a great legacy of Christian goodwill.

Here again, if we are to be rational, we cannot ignore the problems of Christian mission in the world. Helping the poor might *feel* good, but it flies in the face of the most reasonable principles of natural law. The odd and outdated belief in the sanctity of life prevents Christians from viewing humans as part of a larger web that is open to the forces of evolution and adaptation. A species improves and becomes more vigorous as the genetically deficient, the lame, the weak and the elderly within a population are allowed to die off. In fact, much of our misery as a species is linked directly to the fact that we preserve the elements of our species that are least desirable, all in the name of God.

Perhaps ideas like compassion, mercy and grace, though outside the realm of logic, have a special place in our culture. Maybe there are reasons that go beyond rationalism which make legitimate belief in something beyond the five senses. Speaking of grace, what could be more absurd? Grace argues that God forgives all sins regardless of the cost. Grace wipes the slate clean when we would most enjoy seeing someone get what they deserve. At least karma is just—what we do now determines what happens to us later. If we seek to harm, we will be harmed. Karma makes sense because it keeps us from harming others and insures justice to those who have been wronged. Grace gives up the right to justice. As tourists, this is difficult to justify in the face of logic. Grace argues that we receive the favor of God even when we don't deserve it. All are forgiven when they turn to God, regardless of their past. All the Hitlers of the world could have repented in their dying moments and made it to heaven while a good man who wanted nothing to do with God would not. Grace, unmerited favor, is not reasonable.

As tourists seeing things for the first time, the gospel and the manner it was delivered to the world are hard to understand. As the truth, Christianity should be something easy and accessible to everyone. The very opposite seems to be true. There are many obstacles to faith that seem to be placed purposely. One family is chosen as God's people. One very small and backward nation receives the Messiah. Amid several competing world religions Christianity enters with no convincing proof of its supremacy. Could God have given us a clearer global presentation, with every nation hearing and understanding, of what he is doing and what he wants of us?

Instead, we have the New Testament, a collection of books that chronicle the life of Jesus, who, living in the back country of a very small nation in a remote corner of the Roman Empire, entrusted his message to twelve uneducated men. Jesus left no book, no guide and no ongoing, reproducible miracle to point to. All we can do is trust the testimony of someone who heard it from someone who heard it from someone that he rose from the dead. This message took centuries to spread, during which entire nations, whole swaths of the planet, never even heard of the name of Jesus. And then, once the church did achieve supremacy over parts of the earth, it was filled with corruption, waged war on other religions and kept the Bible in a language foreign to most people. Is this a logical way to get the word out?

Even if the distribution of the gospel was efficient and instantaneous, just trying to make sense of the message is difficult at times. Jesus purposely spoke in parables, which make his message hard to pin down. Time and time again we read the disciples were confused about what Jesus was saying. Even Jesus comments on his counterintuitive approach to preaching:

He said, "The knowledge of the secrets of the kingdom of

God has been given to you, but to others I speak in parables,
so that,

   'though seeing, they may not see;

   though hearing, they may not understand.' " (Luke 8:10)

What a strange method for a message that is so crucial. If this is
the purpose of parables, to make the truth more difficult to find
rather than less difficult, how does this help spread the gospel
with clarity?

So let's review: The way Christians act is weird. The theology
is illogical. The message seems absurd. The ethics run counter to
what is natural. Morality seems like an arbitrary system of right
and wrong. In fact, it seems biblical morality seems to restrict or
prohibit those things most vital and natural to who we are. Christianity seems to neuter humans rather than let us express the ex-
tent of our humanity. The message is conveyed in a confusing and
counterproductive way.

We would be crazy to follow a faith that has so many logical
inconsistencies. But perhaps madness is a matter of perspective.
When we are dealing with something so broad as the existence of
God, how can we be sure we have the correct view? Wouldn't
God be so completely different from us that he would strain our
logic? Because humans have an affinity for reason, wouldn't a
reasonable faith seem like a human construct? I like to think that
faith is something we'd have to be crazy to embrace. But whose
craziness am I referring to?

Rodney Clapp mentions "holy madness" in his book *A Peculiar
People*. Clapp refers to the movie *Serpico*, in which a New York
City police officer is pressured by his peers to accept bribes as a
part of his job. Since he is the only one who doesn't take bribes,
he winds up feeling like a criminal. The entire thing is upside
down. His girlfriend tries to support him through this disorient-

ing time by telling him an old story. The citizens of a kingdom drank from a polluted well and went crazy. Since the king was the only one who didn't drink from the well (and was consequently the only one sane), his subjects resisted his rule. They insisted that he drink from the same water they had. When the king finally succumbed, the subjects were delighted that he too became "sane." Sanity is determined by the behavior of the group. Since insanity was the norm, the king drank the poison and everyone regarded him as sane.

When we think of truth, we usually have one standard to evaluate it—logic. But if God exists, there is a standard outside of logic—a different "normal" by which to evaluate truth. Clapp summarizes the impact this has on those who believe: "Like that king, Christians have a source of water other than the world's. . . . So it is against great odds and severe resistance that we are called to a holy madness." The great resistance we encounter in this world either pushes us to accept what the world views as true or to embrace a holy madness. Clapp goes on to quote Robert Inchausti, who believes that "to be insane is to reject the given universals [and where the world turns things upside down] holy madness is the only true sanity."[1]

Clapp is writing in the context of morality, but the same principle applies in our discussion. We are crazy to believe in something so clearly absurd. The only sane thing to do is to drink from the same well that everyone else does, which leads us to believe that only what we can see and sense is what is real. Or is it a matter of perspective? Do we limit our understanding by believing that only what we can experience through our senses or process in our minds determines truth? What lies beyond the limits of our five senses, and is it possible to gain knowledge of this Other? How do we begin to appreciate something beyond our minds? We start by dropping the need to make everything make sense.

3

STOP MAKING SENSE

A FEW YEARS BACK I MADE A DISCOVERY in a grocery store. After I tell you about it, you will never look at the dairy aisle in the same way again. Actually it was my brother Jim who showed me the difference. If you look closely at packages of cheese in the grocery store, there are real cheeses like Camembert, Gouda or Vermont Sharp White Cheddar. These are the kind of cheeses you serve with expensive crackers, and you get cranky when someone else takes the last slice. These kind of cheeses take years to make and come complete with enzymes and flavor (and the ability to get moldy pretty quickly). They are the real thing, though—the best stuff.

In the same dairy section of the supermarket, though, there is something called "pasteurized processed cheese food." If you look too quickly you will miss that it is not actually cheese, but cheese food. Cheese *food?* There is a difference between cheese and cheese *food.* My thought is, if they need to tell you it is food, it isn't worth eating. Can you imagine if there were steak and then there were *ground and mechanically separated beef food.* Sounds gross. Essentially, certain cheese manufacturers got together and said, "Cheese is expensive, cheese gets moldy too quickly, and it is a pain to cut into slices." So they made this stuff that sort of tastes like cheese, fits in nice little plastic wraps, costs half as much and lasts about a hundred years in your refrigerator. Real cheese is made out of milk and takes a long time to develop its flavor. Cheese food is plastic.

Actually, pasteurized processed cheese food is 47 percent water. It is made of oil, water, gelatin, emulsifying agents, and mold inhibitors like sorbic acid and sodium sorbate (yum). When I think of the good cheese, I think of people in Switzerland named Johann who live in the Alps and regard cheese-making as an art form. Cheese food, on the contrary, reaches the store without ever touching human hands and can be made with a chemistry set. Cheese food is a lot friendlier to the consumer, but let's face it—they took the cheese out of it.

I think of this kind of plasticity when I hear people trying to force faith into making sense. If we are not careful, we can rob Christianity of its distinctive flavor. To make it more friendly to the consumer, we have robbed it of its difficulties. "Look! 100 percent faith that is convenient and easy to figure out—*and it fits entirely in your brain!*" No, faith is difficult; it is hard to believe and requires risk and effort to grasp. Faith is wild and demands a lot from us as rational beings. It requires humility and forces us to accept that we are not as smart as we think. Faith takes us on a crazy journey. By trying to make sense of things we bend the absurdities of faith to logic and make the way smooth. It is easy to believe in a faith that has been explained, but how likely are we to believe in a faith that violates everything we think we know about truth and reason? The real question isn't whether Christianity is a reasonable faith, but whether we are willing to believe it when it isn't. Is your faith strong enough to stop making sense?

This is not to say that faith doesn't have a logic to it. It does, but it is very different than the logic we are used to. At this point, however, it is important to notice how moldable and, in some ways, *subjective* reason can be. In the last chapter we looked at the irrational nature of faith. Now we will examine how limited logic is.

We tend to hold on to this idea that logic is something handed to us from on high, that logic and rationality are the unassailable means by which we evaluate what is true and not true about the universe. For a variety of reasons we forget that reason is something constructed within our minds. In order to move through the world we inhabit, we have to observe patterns, see similarities and make forecasts about the way things behave. When we use the word *make* in the phrase "making sense of things," we forget that *making* is in fact the key verb—we manufacture reason, it is not revealed to us. The American philosopher William James talked about the kind of mental bending that takes place when we try to make sense of things. James was a believer in pragmatism, an American-made form of philosophy that beat the French to postmodernism by almost half a century.

James argued that truth is something humans *make* from their experiences.[1] For example, if it is January in America it *makes sense* that it is cold outside. It is a truth that January and cold weather go together. "January is cold" is a true statement. This makes sense to us especially if we live in New York City. Of course it would make no sense to go outside in your bathing suit (although I am sure it has happened more than a few times in New York City). If someone went outside in a bathing suit in the middle of January, we would say they are crazy because bathing suits in January don't fit our way of thinking. January and cold go together, therefore a twenty-five degree day on January 1 in New York City *makes sense*. It fits the sense data stored in our memories.

For James, however, cold and January are truths that we have manufactured. Just think of it: the idea of cold really does not exist outside the human experience. *Cold* is just a word we have given to atoms that travel at a slow speed. To prevent skin damage our skin has nerve endings that warn us when these atoms move too slowly. The result is the human experience arbitrarily called "cold." The same is true of fast-moving atoms; heat can cause burns on our skin. Be that as it may, it is enough to understand that the idea of cold is a human-centered phenomenon that has no bearing on the world outside of our own minds. Essentially, we *make* truth because of the effect certain events have on us.

For example, the idea that "January is cold" isn't true in a place like Sydney, Australia. Wearing a heavy coat in January would be ridiculous there, but wearing a bathing suit and cooking on the grill is normal. Completely different perspectives on the weather are evidenced in the northern and southern hemispheres. January in Sydney is like July in New York.

Something only makes sense because it fits into a certain way of looking at the world, not necessarily because that is the way the world truly is. Our point of view is key. Truth, for James, comes from perspective.

It is actually an intriguing thing to realize that reason is not something out there but is something we build within our minds. James argued that we forge truths from the circumstances we encounter in our lives—not the other way around. In short, reason is not something that we encounter (like a thing awaiting discovery) but something we invent. This is intriguing because it opens up a new way of looking at the world—is January inherently cold and I just take notice of it, or does *my* experience of January create something I believe to be true? This is a pretty deep thought—what is the basis of something I call true? Is it true because of some external measure of truth? Are things true because they are reasonable to begin with or is it more likely that my mind makes sense of things in order to manipulate my world better? If sense is not something we find in the world but something our nerve endings deliver to our minds, then truth is not something out there but rather inside our minds. *Truth is not grasped but manufactured.*

So Protagoras was right: "Of all things the measure is Man."[2] Humans have measured and assigned meaning to all things. And this has a lot of implications for the way we look at things. For example, time is a human construct. Admittedly, the idea of time is a little scary. How can that be a human product? Think about it: were seconds discovered? No one crawled into a cave and unearthed a book that described how long a second is. No, a long time ago someone attempted to standardize the passage of time and called the smallest unit a "second." It is suspiciously close to the duration of a heartbeat. Sixty heartbeats make a minute, and sixty minutes make an hour and so on. We have invented the measure of time. Time is something that comes from us, not from somewhere out there. We created it. Regardless of its origin, it was manufactured.

How about numbers? Some people have made mathematics into a religion, as if the discovery of truth lies in math formulas. Sorry to demystify it, but humans created the decimal system too. Isn't it interesting that we have a numerical system based on ten digits, and we have ten fingers? If we had fourteen or twenty fingers, how would we count? It is a fascinating question; perhaps we would have completely different sets of mathematics and physics —the same rules, just different figures. The decimal system and counting in base ten are systems that we have created, not discovered.

Think of all the areas that we have projected ourselves onto the world. A meter comes very close to the stride of a person walking. The liter comes from a region of the world where wine (and the wine bottle, which amounts to the volume of a liter) comes from.

It changes the way we look at the world when we realize that things like decimals, kilometers, liters and seconds are not God-given measurements. They are invented. Their creation comes from our very limited experience in this world. We do not discover something about the universe when we measure it; we create meaning that we can understand. We project ourselves onto matter and call it knowledge. We *make* sense.

Wine and winter weather aside, our active minds notice patterns and create conditions that are predictable and fit nicely into categories. We call this mental activity "making sense of things." There are other ways that we see this at work as well. Our eyes are fooled by optical illusions because the mind tries to resolve things that don't make sense.

Look at figure 3.1. The smile on the fat man's face looks smaller than the thin man's, though they are the same length. Our mind purposely throws out information that does not fit into a preconceived way of thinking. In the process of figuring things out, the mind makes an error because it "makes sense." It is presenting us with incorrect information to make it more reasonable. Sometimes our mind sees things that were never there to begin with.

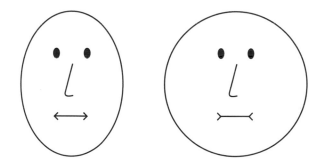

Figure 3.1.

This same kind of mental actvty can be found in a sntnce even though sevral of the letters are mssing. While we can read sentences and entire paragraphs like this, computers can't. Our mind is actively making sense of things—even when there isn't enough information. This was Immanuel Kant's argument about what is real and what is merely in our heads (paraphrasing him, of course). According to Kant, the mind brings a certain way of looking at the phenomena it observes in the world. It imposes a certain order on the world that is not really there. It maps out the world, projecting the way it envisions things onto the world in order to help us manipulate the world and move through it with ease. This may be helpful for us who simply want a world that makes sense, but it is helpful to know that this is a reality constructed on subjective human experience. And this makes us rethink a critique of faith based solely on reason.

Looking at reason this way should cause us to question ourselves. I wonder, what other things are our minds wrong about? Is it possible that humans have identified as reasonable and logical those things that we can grasp, and everything else that doesn't fit inside that very narrow box has been designated as nonsense? Imagine what implications that has for things like faith. Since we can't make "sense" of faith, it becomes a fairy tale, not real, useless, something that would be nice if it were true. But what if faith just *seems* absurd because the mind can't readily grasp it?

But how do we know? If the mind sifts through information and presents to us only the stuff that helps us move through the world, how would we know what we are missing? We easily fall into the trap of believing that the things we observe through the five senses are all there is to know, when in fact it is all that we are able to *make sense of.* It becomes a vicious circle.

What can we know and how do we know we know it? This question is at the center of the scientific method, a series of techniques used to make sure scientific study is uniform and trust-worthy. The method was not discovered, it was created over cen-turies by such notables as Thales, Aristotle, Francis Bacon and Charles Pierce (among others). Bacon borrows heavily from a lesser-known Portuguese doctor, Francisco Sanches, who penned an arcane but very foundational work, *Quod Nihil Scitur (That Nothing Is Known)*. Sanches's conclusion about gaining knowledge marks the beginning of the scientific method. Since humans can-not really know the nature of things, we have to have a working foundation on which some form of knowledge is based. He delin-eated a series of steps by which careful empirical research and cautious judgment could help develop ideas about how the world works, which he termed "el metodo universal de las ciencias."[3] Once again, this method was not handed to us from heaven. Sanches was attempting to give us a starting point for establishing what we can know by the senses. It was a stab in the dark—a best guess. "This would not lead, as his contemporary Francis Bacon thought, to a key to knowledge of the world. But it would allow us to obtain the best information available."[4]

The scientific method is a workbench on which our mind ac-tively attempts to arrange things into patterns that help us move through the world. Those things that hold no promise of fitting into the arrangement, that make no sense, are discarded. Those things that make sense are part of what we call "real" or "true," while things that are nonsense are rejected.

So science is based on a series of human ideas regarding what qualifies as true. And this doesn't sound religious to you? Truth, for science, is that which fits into our system of knowing. One of the central questions of this book is whether faith is actually *more real* because of its inability to fit into the things that we know. Think about this for a moment. What if the truest things in the world are those that are most elusive? In some sort of strange, paradoxical way perhaps the most logical thing about faith is its apparent irrationality.

But instead of embracing this change of perspective, many Christians desire instead to stuff Christianity into the small container of reason. These are the types who argue for the scientific accuracy of Genesis—that the earth is relatively young or that dinosaurs are spoken of in the Bible. Their work is valiant but unnecessary. As if science alone defines what can and can't be true, these brave Christians work endlessly to try to sew up every last detail of faith to fit within the human constructs of truth. It would be interesting to figure out why the Old Testament people of Genesis 1–11 lived so long. But it seems awfully forced to try to resolve the issue by claiming, as Isaac Vail did, that a water canopy covered the earth and prolonged the life of its inhabitants.[5] Trying to force the Scriptures into the explainable has all the allure of fake cheese.

People are hungry for something, but not arguments that seem forced. Why else has atheism become so popular in a postmodern age known for its spirituality? A stream of bestselling books by atheists show how faith lacks any credible evidence. This of course has brought about a response from Christians arguing for evidence of God. These arguments are an ideational Ping-Pong match between Christians and atheists, which make the rest of us uneasy.

If we believe the ultimate truth about reality lies outside of our grasp, how can someone as limitless as God (if we really believe this) make sense to us? This is a hard transition for many Christians to make. Perhaps we have been under the influence of the age of reason for too long. Many Christians feel impelled to *justify* what they believe. Many Christian conversations are really intellectual discussions about the credibility of the gospel or the historical support for the faith. We attempt to persuade people to believe. Many believers have exchanged their privileged role of disciple for apologist, as if Jesus needs a lawyer in the court of human opinion.

It reminds me of a short story by Ray Bradbury. In this story a captain of a spaceship lands on Mars and discovers a whole town of people that heard of the humans' arrival but remain indifferent. Incredulous that he, his crew and human achievement should be overlooked, the captain demands to know what could be more impressive than reaching another planet. A person from the town informs them that Jesus came the day before, and the whole town is captivated by his words and miracles. The captain is a skeptic, so he demands proof of the miracles. Hearing testimony that someone was healed, he brushes it aside as lacking evidence. Someone then shows him a painting of the boy before the healing. The captain's response is typical. "What's this?" he says. "Anyone could have painted someone's lame arm, this proves nothing."[6]

The captain begins to search for evidence among the townspeople and eventually seeks an audience with Jesus himself. His lack of faith in their testimony, however, serves as a turning point in the story. The people of the town look at each other and know that this is a person who will never understand the depth of what they have experienced. His refusal to accept their testimony is what leads to his downfall. Their leader decides to dismiss the captain by telling him that the Jesus he is looking for is gone. The captain goes back to his ship vowing to find Jesus on other worlds. As the captain takes off, the townspeople look up in disappointment. Their assessment is that even if the captain were to meet Jesus, he still wouldn't believe. As the ship's shadow disappears, they go back to see the Jesus that the captain wasn't looking for.

The townspeople represent a rare Christian. Imagine a Christianity that was finally freed from the perennial struggle to *prove* itself to skeptics and just shine in all of its bizarre splendor. What if it didn't feel the weight of having to "make sense"? Imagine the truth being conveyed without worrying how people will take it. This becomes a real test of our faith. Can we believe in it without feeling the weight to prove it? Can we talk about it without the need to justify or make sense of it?

Let's leave cheese-making to those that are good at it.

4

TWO-DIMENSIONAL

EXISTENCE

FAITH IS NOT THE ONLY THING that is absurd; it turns out that reason has its limits as well. Let's go back a little bit.

There you are: curled up, warm, eyes closed, napping. Not a care in the world. Everything you need is at your fingertips. All you need to eat, all you need to drink—taken care of. No need to work, no pain or discomfort. You are at peace with everything. No worries. No anxiety. Just the gentle swaying and rhythm of a heartbeat.

And then, BOOM!

Muscles contract and push you down a narrow corridor. The movements are sudden and forceful. Your head is squeezed into the shape of a cone and you make first contact with a cold room, bright lights and weird noises. A doctor cuts your lifeline. For the first time, icy cold air fills your lungs, which is a strange feeling. You hear loud crying—the very first time you are using your own voice. Quickly you are wrapped in a blanket. Lights hurt your eyes. Sound is now clear and distinct. Before you can get a handle

on what has happened, hands are all over you, your first bath. A
nurse inserts a bulb into your nose and mouth to suck mucus from
your airways. You are then placed on the metal surface of a scale—
you feel the weight of your body on your back, another first. And
if you are a male, the prospect of circumcision looms on the horizon. Oh joy.

Then you are handed to your mother, your father and eventually everyone who visits the hospital room. This makes you desperately want to go back to where you were safe and warm.
Camera flashes, blurry images of people, strange noises. Since all
of your senses are new, you have just begun to adjust to hearing,
seeing and smelling. In the first few months of life everybody
gawks at you and makes funny noises. Everything you see is a
first: strange faces, household pets, baby mobiles. All the stimu-
lation must be frightening at first. Perhaps this is why no one
remembers these jarring first days of life.

Leaving the warmth, softness and safety of the womb is quite
jarring. Over the course of time, a similar momentous leap occurs
as we become aware of ourselves. Not only do we move into our
body, we move into our minds, a very scary and draining process.
Sleep helps, and there is a lot of it over the first couple of months.
Over time, however, we begin to rely on our senses for information. We start to understand that a dark room means nighttime,
which is for sleeping. We learn that hunger pangs lead to crying,
which leads to milk. Our ears deliver the tender words of a
mother, and we come to understand that being held is reassuring
and soothing. Cold bathwater makes us cry. Diapers get smelly
and uncomfortable. That mobile above the crib is fascinating.
The perfume from Aunt Dorothy is . . . strong.

The information our senses bring us becomes the basis for how
we interact with the world. Not only do they tell us what is happening in the world, but they interact with our memory and will

to produce actions—the things we do in order to get what we want. When we feel cold, we start to cry. Crying brings someone with a blanket, and we are warm. What we sense helps us make decisions on how to interact with the world. Our senses and memory are beginning to help us formulate basic reasoning skills.

As our brains develop, those senses become the building blocks of reason. We learn that when we are hungry, we cry, and we are then fed. When we smell that strong perfume, we cry and fidget, and we are released from that odor. We learn that our senses help us move through the world successfully. As a young child, a bee sting aggravates nerve endings in our skin and delivers the message of pain. Mere sense experiences would mean getting stung again, but sense interacts with our memory, and whenever we see a black and yellow flying insect we automatically get nervous and cautiously back away. Voilà! Sense and reason have saved the day. We have learned something. And so it goes that sense combines with memory to give rise to reason and knowledge, because we build knowledge from the things we remember.[1] We remember the things that we sense. So sense data leads to reason, and it all works together to help us navigate through the world.

We don't often reflect on what a gift sense and reason are. We take it for granted and project it onto the world around us. We assume that human rationality is capable of leading us to all the answers. In the same way a fish assumes the entire universe is made of and defined by the physics of water, we have made reason the final truth about all things. While it is true that for fish, water is the definitive element of living in the sea, the sea is not all there is. Similarly, the world around us has a structure that can be investigated through rational principles, but it too has its limits.

We don't really think about the limits of reason and sense experience, and why should we? Reason works; it's what is real. Everything we understand about the nature of things comes through using our senses to observe the world. We can even make predictions about what will happen. When we see clouds and feel a humid wind stir, we can reasonably predict that it will rain. When we feel nauseated and begin to sweat, we can reasonably predict that we will soon be sick. And when we see that the bodies of all dead beings decay (and that nothing we have ever seen has ever come back to life), we can reasonably predict that there is no afterlife. You may tell me there is a God, but I have never seen him with my eyes. If it defies reason (e.g., is nonsense), it can't exist.

Our senses are wonderful things that allow us to succeed and move through the world. For example, our eyes are impressive sense organs that are finely calibrated to the human body. Because of their fine calibration, however, they are limited. We can't see the ultraviolet patterns on flowers that bees see. Bees have senses finely suited to their needs, just as we do. This is also true for the other sense abilities that we have. We can't hear the high frequencies that dogs hear. Their senses are finely calibrated to their dog tasks. Humans are inferior to dogs in hearing. And dogs' sense of smell is much more acute than ours.

Does this mean we are inferior to dogs? Of course not, but it does mean that our senses paint a very different picture of the world for us. Our experience is drastically different from the information gathered by dogs and bees. For example, dogs sniff other dogs for reasons we don't understand. (Thankfully, we don't engage in this behavior!) Humans primarily use sight to recognize other humans. If we could get more information by sniffing them, I suppose we would do that.

Bees convey information by returning to the hive and doing a special dance. From the information conveyed in the dance, other bees know where to find a source of food. Bee dancing is a kind of language. For example, if the source of food is less than fifty feet away, bees dance in circles.[2] Humans tend to transfer information through speaking and writing. If we could convey more information through dancing, perhaps we would dance instead of talk. (With my dance abilities, I would be an illiterate bee.)

It is striking to see how limited human senses are. Compared to certain animals, the range of our senses seems small. But one thing is certain. *The way that we see and interpret the world is a direct result of the abilities of our senses.*

Once, as a child, I was walking with my dog, Brandy, through a field when she became tense and begin to growl. I was oblivious, but it was obvious that something had caught my dog's attention. A few minutes later I discovered that a very large dog was more than slightly annoyed that I was walking through his field. With only human sense abilities I had no idea what danger awaited, but Brandy was on alert and ready to defend. Brandy's senses and response helped me avoid danger.

We see this in other animals. Birds scurry about getting ready for an advancing storm. Cows tend to sit down before it rains. Do they sense that rain is coming? Perhaps they are preserving a nice dry bed? For whatever reason, it is obvious that different sense capabilities promote different reasoned responses. Sense and reason are linked. A limited range of senses affects our behavior and our reason.

We scoff at bird brains that lead birds to fly into sliding glass doors. But don't humans have similar lapses of judgment? It is exactly this blind spot that leads us to forget how frail logic and reason are.

But if sense and reason are linked, we can't claim to know anything more than our senses tell us. Bertrand Russell, Nobel Prize–winning philosopher, mathematician, logician and author of scores of books (among them *Why I Am Not a Christian),* said it more lucidly: "Man can't know what science can't discover."[3] Essentially, Russell confines all human thought to those things that we can directly experience through our senses. All that we can know is only what we or others can directly observe. According to this, if we were to imagine all of human knowledge we could portray it as two axes: the Y axis represents all that we can directly sense or experience and the X axis represents that which we can learn through someone else's experiences that can be demonstrated to us through the senses (see fig. 4.1).

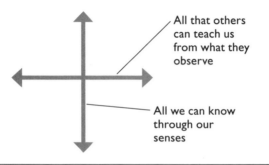

All that others can teach us from what they observe

All we can know through our senses

Figure 4.1. The means of knowledge

Of course this is a huge area of knowledge. From these axes we have been able to create vaccines that save lives, vessels that fly in the air and literature that has enriched our lives for centuries. Humanity has greatly benefited from the huge expanse of knowledge that human reason has afforded us. To not give reason its place of honor would be ridiculous. Even some of the great Christian theologians have attributed our *imago dei* of Genesis 1:26-27 as our abilities to reason.

However, though Russell's quote is an accurate view of human perception, it reflects a very limited view of knowledge. If we believe that truth can be discovered only through the senses, then we live in a very small world. *How can we think that reality is discovered only through our five senses?* Perhaps Russell's statement should be "Science can't know what humans can't sense." This is more accurate and to the point. Scientific inquiries are relegated to the realm of the senses and human reason, but Russell is clear: Humans can't know what science can't discover. This form of knowledge is flat, comprising only what our minds can process.

Flat knowledge is devoid of depth. The X and Y axes are fed by the senses and shaped into reason, but they don't carry the full spectrum of knowing. There is knowledge that is available to us that runs outside the senses. As an example of how flat reason is, outside of my office window there is a beautiful cardinal that likes to pay me visits throughout the day. Sometimes I stop what I am doing and study the bird, marveling at its superior ability to fly. I see this graceful and wonderful creature alight on a branch outside my window and am awestruck—until it does the most stupid thing I think a creature can do. With all the fortitude of a commando storming the beach, it musters its strength and flies straight into my window. The first time I saw this I flinched and worried that the poor little guy might be dead. But he got back on his little bird legs and flew off. Usually within minutes he is back to try it again.

Is he upset with me? Did I look at him the wrong way? Is he trying to attack the reflection he sees of himself? Is he tired of being outside and wants to come in? Perhaps he sees this as a shortcut around the building. I think of all of these possibilities until I am faced with the most deflating thought. For all the majesty and wonder this bird possesses, though he can soar with grace, he still has a bird brain. Bird brains make stupid decisions. How can we expect any more from a creature that has a brain the size of a raisin? Bird brains give rise to bird reason.

This helps me understand something better. The amount of a creature's sense bandwidth and the relative size of its brain produces its amount of reason. Bird senses work with bird brains to produce bird behavior. This is true for every species. The amount of information they have available to them plus the processing speed of the brain always equals the reasoning capabilities of the animal.

So if we can agree that bird brains make bird logic (and bird logic is pretty ridiculous at times), wouldn't it be safe to assume that all creatures have this same amount of self-limitation? Or are humans the only creatures this does not apply to? Something doesn't sound right with that. The simple fact is that humans are not above the rule that sense and reason are linked. Because they are linked, limited sense capabilities and limited brain power equals limited reasoning abilities. Since reason is so intimately linked with sense capabilities, we need to come to a very uncomfortable conclusion about reason or our ability to make sense of things: *Because our sense abilities are rather narrow, so is our logic.* If reason and logic are built solely on the senses, than we have to conclude that reason and logic are as finite and limited as humans are limited. Reason is stunted by the limits of being human.[4] What is true for the bird is true for the human—just in different measures.

Now some would object to this conclusion on the basis that human reason has allowed us to build machines that are able to perceive things outside of our sense range. We have developed electron microscopes and radiation telescopes and such. Birds can't even develop the technology that would reveal it is flying into glass. We have become, in the words of Sigmund Freud, *prosthetic gods*, able to go beyond the limits of our senses and expand the spectrum of our reason into superhuman (even godlike) dimensions. Since we have expanded our sense abilities to see beyond their normal range, we can have more insight and therefore superior reasoning abilities.

Well, yes, in some ways we have pushed the limits of our senses' abilities to recognize certain things. For example, we have developed cameras that can see ultraviolet waves of light as a bee can, but this is only translation. The bee senses it as native to its abilities and lives within the ultraviolet world. The monitor I have in front of me that displays ultraviolet light translates this information to my eyes within the visible spectrum. I am not truly seeing ultraviolet wavelengths. The computer senses ultraviolet radiation and translates it into visible light as purple streaks on my monitor. So while we have an adaptation of what a bee can see, it is something taken out of its native environment and translated to our environment. These become analogies for what is real, which is not knowing in the truest sense.

So while the plane of human knowledge is impressive and seemingly limitless in potential, it is in the same breath profound in its limitations. For all that we can know and attempt as humans, human-based reason and logic fall flat because of a major flaw: the inability to tell us *why*. This may seem ridiculously obvious, but the best our senses can do is passively observe. Human senses are really just devices that monitor the outside world. All they do is give us data about our environment. They answer "What is taking place?" not "Why is this taking place?" The "what" is apprehended by the senses, whereas the "why" is conveyed to us through the revealing of a motive. Aristotle saw the limits of reason in his *Metaphysics:* "Again, we do not regard any of the senses as Wisdom; yet surely these give the most authoritative knowledge of particulars. But they do not tell us the 'why' of anything—e.g. why fire is hot; they only say that it is hot."[5]

Of course we know that there is really no such thing as hot or cold—just the relative speed of atoms in an object. But our nerves use this information and give us sensations that warn us if we are about to handle something that may damage our skin. In the same way, there really is no green, just a certain length light wave not reflected from an object. "Smooth" is a certain way that molecules are arranged in an object that stimulates our nerve endings in a different way than what we describe as "rough." Outside of a human, heat, cold, color and texture are not really there. And these are just some of the many ways that our brains work with our senses to create a world specific to the human. Because of the way the mind asserts itself onto the world, we have to question the ability of the senses to really assemble a trustworthy set of facts about the nature of reality. Immanuel Kant put it more academically:

> If we take away the subject (humans), or even only the subjective constitution of our senses in general, then not only the nature and relations of objects in space and time, but even space and time themselves disappear; . . . not only are the raindrops mere appearances, but even their circular (spherical) form, nay, the space itself through which they fall (motion), is nothing in itself, but both are mere modifications or fundamental dispositions of our sensible intuition, whilst the transcendental object remains for us utterly unknown.[6]

Kant is saying that what we know about things is merely the appearance or the surface of things. The senses are an active grid that deliver to our brain a construct of what the world *looks* like, *feels* like and *sounds* like. It projects something we call "real" or "what is really there," when it is actually presenting to us the surface of things—only what is there, not why it is there. The thing in itself—the true essence of what is—will always elude us; our senses are presenting impressions to our mind that are not really there.

This is the most unsatisfying of all conclusions about reason because our deepest questions are questions of meaning, purpose and intent. Why are we here? What is the purpose of my life? Is there a God and who is he? Reason is unable to answer these questions because reason is built from the senses, which are tied only to those things we observe. We really don't want data and observations. The human pursuit of the deeper questions are not about *how* things work. We don't want appearances, we want reasons *why*. This is where reason and logic fail us. Reason and logic are flat; they only answer the what questions, but we want to know why.

Let me explain. When we are observing something, we can descriptively answer *what* it is by stating what we see. "I see flowers"—question answered. It is obvious to our senses that we see flowers. Science and reason are great at identifying and observing *what* is there. We could even ask how. How did they get there? Maybe we bought them from the florist. Perhaps they grew there. We could even say someone sent them as a gift. These are reasonable answers to a specific question because they deal with what we observe.

Where reason fails is in answering *why* it is there. So *why* are the flowers there? There are many levels to answering this question that go beyond the senses. The flowers may be there because I just came back from the garden and want a nice arrangement on the table. They may be there because I am in the proverbial doghouse and need to apologize to my wife. These answers are only discovered by seeking the intent behind putting flowers on the table. Knowing why they are there goes beyond my senses. These answers are conveyed by the will of a person. And such revelation is often surprising. Our answer about the flowers ultimately comes from Aunt Gertrude, who enters through the back door with her gardening gloves on and announces she is staying for the next two weeks. (Perhaps we are better left in the dark after all.)

What is certain is that our senses are limited—answers to our why questions are provided through the disclosure of a person. And this kind of revelation is just as valid a source of truth as description is. This is true in looking at faith as well.

The disconnect between what we can observe and what we discover through intentions leads us in one of two directions. I either know the limits of logic and turn to an answer that is beyond my reasoning abilities, or I despair that all I can know is all I can see and sense.

When someone reveals something, he or she draws back the curtain on its purpose. Someone explains why the object is there. The problem with revelation is that there is no proof; we have to accept the person's word. Ideally our senses (the data aspect) work with revelation (the relational aspect) to give us knowledge that is full, what we might call the truth. When our senses tell us the setting, someone reveals to us the purpose or intent, and both act together to give us the truth. One without the other is incomplete.

And this is the continual weakness of science. We can know what happened up to a millionth of a second before the big bang, but it will never take the place of knowing why it was there to begin with. At heart, we are not satisfied with forensics; we want to know *why*, which always conveys someone's will. Because of that, science will never be able to answer the question why—as long as it is tied only to sense observations. This is our second conclusion about natural reason: *Reason only answers what; it doesn't answer why.*

Let's return to those flowers on the table. If we ask a series of questions about why the flowers are there from a purely scientific perspective, we essentially get nowhere. Science is great for what but horrible at why. Let's see why.

- *Why are the flowers there?* Because flowers come from plants.
- *Why do flowers come from plants?* Because plants grow from seeds.
- *Why do plants grow from seeds?* Because seeds germinate and grow.
- *Why do seeds germinate and grow?* Because the seed casing softens when watered.

- *Why does it soften?* So that the small radical (little root) can emerge and dig into the soil.

- *Why does it emerge?* So it can draw water, resume growth for the little embryonic plant and push through the soil.

- *Why does it push through the soil?* Because by pushing through the soil, it is able to unfurl its small leaves and power the plant.

- *Why does it power the plant?* Because leaves change sunlight into food for the plant for it to grow bigger.

- *Why does it grow?* Because that's what plants do.

This is a fine example of what the limits of reason are. Essentially it comes down to "That's what it does. Now go away and stop bothering me." Someone who wants to know the *purpose* of flowers will be disappointed by reason, which can only tell us what it senses. Notice each answer to why only tells us what seeds *do*. It never tells us the purpose of seeds or plants or even embryos. That is because our senses are narrow; all that we can know comes from the things that we can sense. Information anchored in reason is flat.

To answer why, we need to get into the head of someone else who will reveal the intent behind his or her action. This is the third conclusion about the limits of reason. *Reason limits us to remaining inside our own heads.* The funny thing about reason is that it restricts us to the confines of the mind. If we think that the universe is the result of no Mind or Creator, then we are at least consistent. But if we choose to believe that everything we see around us is the result of something beyond the limit of our senses, how can we get at what that is by reason alone? To really know the truth, we have to get outside of our heads.

When we want to know why flowers bloom, we can read an

authoritative botany book about flowers. We could become experts at the division of cells, the way that seeds germinate and how photosynthesis works. But ultimately we have only explored the insides of our own heads, we have only displayed the triumph of our senses. What we have accomplished is really nothing more than satisfying an urge for data.

5

ALL IN YOUR HEAD

IT IS THE END OF THE WORKDAY. I turn out the light in my office and say goodbye to my friend the cardinal, who continues to pound at my window. I shake my head and smile, wondering when I will come into my office to find shattered glass and a very proud cardinal flying around the room.

What I would give to morph into a cardinal, fly up to my friend and explain that he doesn't need to give himself a headache every day by careening into my office window. There are other more productive things he can be doing with his time. I wonder if it would make a difference to him if I took him by the wing and flew him around to the other side of the building. Maybe I could fly him to a glass-making factory and explain the properties of glass and what *transparency* means. Can birds even understand *transparency*? As an optimist I like to think that if I had the command of bird language for a few moments I could make a difference in his life. But for now, he is stuck in his ways, and no one outside of his brain can convince him otherwise.

I get in my car and travel home. As I pull up to a red light, I see a big dog looking at me from the back of a truck. I like dogs like some people like babies. I love to run around and play fetch with them, but when they start slobbering, it's time for the owner to take them back. I love dogs, really, it's just that I'm used to low-impact dogs. Tell them to sit and they sit; ask them to go outside and they go outside. Once they start jumping all over me, game over.

Well, the big dog in the truck was staring at me, and I made the mistake of looking at it. As soon as our eyes met, his widened and he stood up and began to bark. I can handle barking from a distance, but there is something about a dog barking at me from a few feet that is annoying; it makes me flinch with each piercing yelp. I tried to smile and calm the dog down. Big mistake. My attention got him barking louder. I don't speak dog, but each bark sounded to me like

Woof! (Translation: "What?")

Woof! W-woof! ("What?" "W-w-what?")

Woof! Woof! Woof! ("What do you have? Gimme what you have! Gimme what you have!")

I kept thinking, *I don't have anything for you. Sit down!*

As I gave more attention to the dog, even negative attention, it was like pouring gasoline on a fire. The louder he got, the more annoying it became—this is why I don't have a dog. Arguing with a dog is like trying to soothe an angry foreigner. You try to slow down and speak louder, but it doesn't help. Here again, if only I could take the form of a dog, come alongside him and bark, "Hey dog, he doesn't have anything for you. He has a cat. Let's go bark at some other guy. I think that one over there has a big bone in the back seat."

Thankfully, the light turned green and I drove on. I love going home. I have three kids and they can't wait to tell me about their day when I arrive. When I walk through the front door, my three-year-old greets me at the door with a huge "Daddy!" and makes me forget all about my day—especially the dog. I love how she throws herself into my arms with joyful abandon. Kids are great like that—fully present in each moment. Of course, being fully present in each moment means that within fifteen minutes she is just as vigorously throwing herself on the floor, upset with her brother. I watch as my wife tries to make her feel better, with no success. Inconsolable, my little girl goes to the crying chair and weeps. (Yes, we have a crying chair—don't ask.) Once again I desire to get inside someone's head. I wish I could be another three-year-old girl, climb up in the chair, stroke her hair and help her out of her sadness.

My frustration with the dog and even the cardinal are understandable. A great barrier separates the human and animal world. As we have seen, not only is communication an issue, but the size of the brain and the ability to reason are barriers as well. This is why it would be helpful to be able to relate to them, to somehow get inside their head. They have no idea of the world outside their limited understanding. The cardinal has no clue what transparency is. The dog has no clue that I really don't like slobbery animals that jump all over you. The limits of their understanding sets limits on their world. The only way to get them to see more would be for someone to reveal it to them from outside of their limited senses.

This idea is congruent with what we have been observing so far. There are things directly accessible to us through our senses. In fact some people, like Russell, think that the only real things are those we can sense. There is a problem with this, though, which becomes evident with the cardinal, the dog and my little girl. When all we rely on is our senses, we run the risk of being trapped in our heads. It becomes a circular argument to say that all there is, is all we can experience. How can we possibly know that unless we are able to get outside of our heads? The limited nature of our senses and the reason that is formed from these senses limits the world we know. In order for us to know more, we need it to be revealed from outside our abilities. Otherwise we remain stuck in our own heads.

A great example of this comes from Richard Dawkins's book *The God Delusion*. As a way to illustrate his ideas on faith, Dawkins likens the activities of a moth to the human preoccupation with religion. As we all know, at night moths are oddly drawn to light. Turn on a porch light on a summer night and there's an instant insect party. Light a torch or candle on the patio and bugs will come. No one is certain why moths (or other insects) circle and eventually dive-bomb into flames.

In his book Dawkins proposes that perhaps moths are wired to travel to and from their homes at night using light as a fixed navigation point. If, on the moth's way to and from finding food, the moon remains at thirty degrees, the moth will find its way to and from home at night.[1] However, Dawkins theorizes that when moths come across a flame, the moth's internal guidance system is tricked and it begins to fly in thirty-degree arcs into the fire, entering a slow spiral to certain death. The moth's natural ability to navigate by the light of the moon is interfered with by an artificial source of light that leads to its death. The event is a parable that Dawkins uses to warn us of the dangers of faith. Essentially, religion and superstition have created a competing flame that has lured us off of our evolutionary courses and caused us all to spiral toward the flames of destruction.

The example that Dawkins uses, however, argues for the opposite of what he suggests, and I am surprised that he didn't catch it. The moon in his example represents how we ought to orient ourselves and navigate through our lives naturally and by the forces of evolution. But the religious manmade fires have drawn us away from truth and represent the greatest human peril. I get it that Dawkins, a scientist, sees faith as a corrupting agent. Without myths and superstitions, we would all be able to fly freely and safely. Religion is a disorienting source of soothing untruths that lure us off our natural path and threaten to undo the advancement of the species. His theory is interesting but there is one problem: *The poor moth was only doing what its senses had programmed it to do.*

Think about this for a second. I know that (relatively speaking) moths are dumb, but you can't blame a moth for having a brain the size of a sesame seed. We shouldn't be so hard on the poor creature. All things considered, the moth is doing the best it can with the equipment it has. In fact, the moth was not led astray by its quest for an afterlife or desire for consolation from a religious crutch. Superstition wasn't what drew the moth off course; it was its reliance on its own senses. What kills the moth is its complete reliance on empirical data. Dawkins's example actually critiques the trustworthiness of the senses. If moths use their moth senses and repeatedly make tragic decisions, how are humans any different?

The example would be proper if the flame were mimicking the light of the moon, as Dawkins paints religious superstition seeking to draw us off course. The moth was not a victim of wish fulfillment or fear of eternal damnation. There were no moth evangelists preaching to them. No *Left Behind: The Moth Edition.* No, in fact, this little insect was a strict and proper moth scientist. The senses of the moth detected light, and this little creature reasoned that light at thirty degrees would get him home. In the end, it was the moth's misplaced reliance on the senses and reason that doomed it.

Since we have already laid out our critique of reason, what could have saved the moth? Perhaps (and I know this sounds absurd) the moth would listen to a buddy? If the moth had someone who had a perspective external to his own (perhaps a moth who had survived the flames), then this experienced moth could warn our moth about the perils of the fire. What if it were possible for a human to step into a moth skin and attempt to persuade the imperiled moth to not enter the flames?

If this were possible, the moth would have to struggle with competing sets of knowledge: (1) what it perceives, and (2) what it is hearing from its buddy. What the moth senses is right in front of him—there is no refuting it. The light, at thirty degrees, is the way home. But the other moth says it's not so. On the one hand, it has what is painfully obvious. On the other, we have the testimony of another moth. What are the chances the moth will make the right decision? In this instance, relational knowledge trumps rational knowledge.

Renowned Notre Dame philosopher and professor of epistemology Robert Audi argues that if all we had for information was our perception, "we would at best be impoverished" because we need others to help us see what we can't.[2] Now let's take that idea one step further. Audi is speaking of someone who comes alongside and *describes* something that we can't see. What if someone came alongside and *revealed* something that we can't see? I want to make a distinction between descriptive truth, which we can understand through reason, and relational truth, which we come to know by revelation.

This principle is as old as language. Remember when you had to take a foreign language in high school? Scary, I know. You learned in Spanish that there were two words for "to know." There is the verb *saber*, which means "to know," as in "I know there is a hole in the window" (Sé que hay un agujero en la ventana), and there is the verb *conocer*, which means "I know him" (Yo lo conozco). One is "I know *it*" and the other is "I know *him*." One form of knowledge describes some*thing*, the other some*one*. The same is true in French (*savoir* and *connaître*), German (*wissen* and *kennen*) and a host of other languages (except English, oddly enough). These languages indicate a real difference between knowledge that we can observe directly in our head and knowledge that comes from another head. Or you might say one is descriptive (of the senses) and the other is relational (not readily observable but revealed). Relational knowledge can be attained from a person, but it can also describe something known from beyond the senses. We can *know* a restaurant (as in where it is), which is descriptive. Then there is the kind of knowledge that says "I *know* that restaurant" (as in "I've been there"); it is in your heart.

Before you start thinking this sounds a little too cutesy, remember that the majority of our lives are concerned with relational truths—the attempt to find out what is in someone else's head. In our friendships, at work and in our families, most of our energies are spent uncovering others' intentions as well as revealing ours. There is a huge difference between the way we react to a friend who got in a car accident from icy road conditions versus being illegally intoxicated. A client might not return phone calls because of personal problems at home or because he doesn't want your services anymore. These kinds of truths go beyond what can be observed; they are revealed in the context of a relationship. It is truth uncovered beyond the senses.

Now of course even these relational truths need to be conveyed through the senses, but that does not make it a rational exercise. For example, when your father puts his arm around you and says, "I am proud of you," the words are conducted through your ear and brain, but the message doesn't need words. Relational truths transcend descriptive data. Intent and revelation of the will are just as important to understanding what is true as data.

In our legal system, intent matters. When someone falls out of a window, it is an accidental death. When someone is pushed, it may be homicide. Now add the detail of a cheating spouse, and the motive begins to become apparent. Intentions are every bit as real as blood stains at a crime scene. Our will provides a much different side of truth than what our senses are able to deliver. And so we need to assign relational truth its proper place. In prior chapters we looked at *what* is true, but more important to humans is *why* things happen. *Why* is just as important as *what*.

In fact, some would say *why* is more important than what. Which would you rather know—the breadth of the galaxy and the number of stars in it, or why the galaxy is here? Some people end their lives because they perceive their lives have no purpose. Some may well know their purpose in life and that is what causes them to consider ending it all. It is obvious that the greater matters of life revolve around the weightier matters of intent and purpose. Regardless, relational truths that are revealed to us are just as true as those that we can observe and describe. I've never heard of a person ending it all because of the specific heat of a molecule or the brightness of a star. *Why* haunts us—not *what*.

The answer to why we are here is elusive, though. The search for truth leaves us empty if all we are doing is using our senses to discover it. That's because the why of truth has to be revealed from something or someone outside of our heads. Descriptive truth, the what, keeps us flying around the flame. Relational truth, which comes from beyond our experience, reveals the why. Descriptive truth is flat, focused on our senses and confined to our heads. The difference between the two is vast. Descriptive truth is rooted in analysis and dissection; it pulls things apart to find what is there. Relational truth interacts with the entire system; it wants to keep things intact so that it can hear the heart of the issue, not just actions.

In the matter of dissection, if we really wanted to know, say a cat, we could split the cat open, pull apart vertebrae and slice open the spinal cord. Tracing this cord to other nerve centers, we would marvel at the wiring of this creature. Not satisfied with just the nervous system, we could examine the cat's amazing muscles in its hind legs. The haunches have a much greater mass than other parts of the creature. Stripping away muscle fiber after muscle fiber we would be amazed at the power they generate. We could open up its throat and look for the source of its purr. The problem with this is that though we have learned a great deal, the cat is dead. Dissection and analysis allow our senses to observe, but they do limit our ability to understand. They are flat and devoid of life.

If I spent the same time with a live cat, I could describe its playfulness, how it always seems to land on its feet. I could smile at the warm sound of it purring on a sunny window sill. I could marvel at the awe-inspiring sight of seeing it jump five times its height. I would not be able to tell you how many quarts of blood run through its circulatory system or what chemicals in its eyes facilitate night vision. Dissection may tell us about a cat's parts, playing with the cat reveals something deeper. Neither source is exhaustive, but this is the point. To only trust in descriptive information and nothing else is so narrow. To ignore the descriptive truth about anything is to forget the impact that knowledge has on us as humans.

Looking at the axes of knowledge (see fig. 5.1), we have already seen that what we know can be represented by a graph of the Y axis (what we can see and sense—our rational experiences) and the X axis (what others have learned through the employment of reason).

We need to visualize a way to imagine revealed truth, a third way of knowing. Revealed truth, the kind of truth that is given to us from another person, is not tied to the observation and description of objects and things. Revealed truth is intangible; through relationship we learn through a person sharing something with us. Since these things tend to lend depth to our lives, let's imagine that the relational—those truths that are revealed to us—comprise the Z axis.

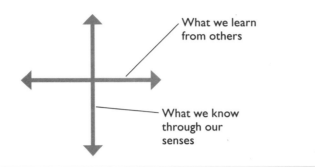

Figure 5.1. The means of knowledge

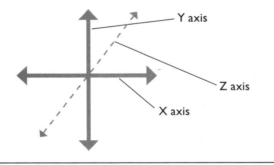

Figure 5.2.

The Z axis in figure 5.2 represents truths conveyed to us that lie beyond observation and description. The Z axis provides depth. It is like walking through an art museum and viewing all the paintings. Perhaps I like them and perhaps I don't. As I go from painting to painting, they all begin to look the same. Descriptively, there is a canvas layered with pigment that creates an image I recognize. I could tell you what I see and maybe what I feel, but I would be no closer to understanding the depth of the painting—the intended purpose of the painting.

But if I grab the nearest museum guide, all kinds of information about the artwork is available to me. When I hear of what

Van Gogh went through in his short and tortured life, the painting *Starry Night* is transformed. The depth of relational truth, the underlying story of his tragic life, reveals to me something beyond what I can see. The truth that is revealed comes from outside of my head and is just as real, and sometimes *more* real, than what my eyes see.

Now we can apply relational truth to our thoughts about faith and God. Let's remember a few things. As we seek to find out what is true, we become disappointed because human reason is actually very limited. Because human reason is so limited, "anything we can't explain needs to be passed over in silence."[3] Which, in the end, is tremendously unsatisfying because *why* is much more important that *what*. In essence, we have dissected the world and rejected the soul in an effort to find what we really seek—depth.

For that we need to look beyond ourselves, to something or someone else. This is where faith appears and offers us an alternative to the flat and lifeless two-dimensional knowledge. God becomes the three-dimensional presence that intersects our two-dimensional world. And I'm not recommending some fuzzy ideas like channeling or some divine mystery that mystics feel. God's space and ours intersect through revelation. Philip Clayton summarizes:

> For if something finite exists, and if the infinite is "excluded" by the finite, then it is not truly infinite or without limit. To put it differently, there is simply no place for finite things to "be" outside of that which is *absolutely unlimited*. Hence an infinite God must encompass the finite world that he has created.[4]

Plainly put, if God is infinite, there is no place in the universe where we can reside outside of him. The Bible puts it in a way that is much more helpful and less pantheistic. The Scriptures present a God who is present in everything, from military campaigns to the personal trials we go through. Through the ages, the consistent thing we see from God is that he is among us:

That night the LORD appeared to him and said, "I am the God of your father Abraham. Do not be afraid, for I am with you; I will bless you and will increase the number of your descendants for the sake of my servant Abraham." (Genesis 26:24)

And the LORD said to Joshua, "Today I will begin to exalt you in the eyes of all Israel, so they may know that I am with you as I was with Moses." (Joshua 3:7)

So do not fear, for I am with you;
    do not be dismayed, for I am your God.
I will strengthen you and help you;
    I will uphold you with my righteous right hand.
(Isaiah 41:10)

Do not be afraid of the king of Babylon, whom you now fear. Do not be afraid of him, declares the LORD, for I am with you and will save you and deliver you from his hands. (Jeremiah 42:11)

And surely I am with you always, to the very end of the age. (Matthew 28:20)

So we search for the truth that comes from outside of our perspective. If we are the bird careening into the window, we need someone to explain to us the futility of what we are doing. The same is true for the dog and my little girl. Someone nearby reveals it to us. And so something sticks out. Relational truth comes to us from outside of ourselves. The truth shows up.

6

GUESS WHO IS AT
THE DOOR

A CERTAIN MAN WHO WORKS in a warehouse was finishing up his shift and getting ready to go home. He had come to work when it was still dark; now it was three in the afternoon, and he was ready to go home and relax. After punching his time card, saying good-bye to some friends and hanging up his hardhat, he got into his car and drove home. There was nothing especially different about this day. The sun was bright, the sky was blue. It was a perfect day to unwind and start thinking about what to do after dinner.

He parked his car outside the garage and walked up the short walkway to his small home in the suburbs. Grabbing his mail, he sorted through it while feeling for the doorknob and walking through the front door. His home is modest, but well kept. As he walked in, he put his jacket over the banister of the stairway directly in front of the small foyer. Then he noticed to his right that the curtain in the living room was billowing from a late-afternoon breeze.

Now this man attends to detail. Things have their place, meals have their times and windows should be shut when you leave the house. The fact that the curtain was being blown by a breeze meant that someone opened a window. With his head slightly cocked, he walked over to see why the window was open, and with slight alarm he observed that the window was not opened, it was broken.

As he stepped back to survey the scene, the snap of glass under his shoe confirmed the fact that the window, at some point during the day, was shattered. Looking across the floor, he searched for clues about what happened. Was it a rock with a note attached from a hate group? Do his neighbors not like warehouse foremen? Perhaps a bird is triumphantly perched somewhere on the second floor. The questions are quickly pushed aside as he notices a tennis ball under a chair on the opposite side of the room. He picked it up and examined it. The questions have narrowed but the mystery is still there: *Why did something or someone put a tennis ball through my window?*

Perhaps it is from the tennis courts down the street. Possible, but you would have to have quite an arm to propel a tennis ball that far. Maybe it fell off a delivery truck of tennis balls. Maybe some students on their way to school got carried away and one of their balls wound up in the front window? All of these ideas are equally plausible and are equally falling short of the one answer our subject is looking for. All he wants to know is, "Why is there a hole in my window?"

Other people would shrug their shoulders, get out the broom and clean up the mess. Taping some cardboard in the window, they would run to the store and replace the glass. Not our man. He wants answers—why is that hole in his window and glass on his floor? This question haunts him. So he calls a friend who is a laboratory forensics instructor, a CSI man, and asks him to come over and examine the scene to give him some answers.

The CSI man arrives and sets to work. Pulling out several instruments from his briefcase, he examines the window. Checking the glass shards, he is able to tell the trajectory of the ball's path. Examining the surface of the ball, he extracts fibers from it and observes them under a microscope. He even studies the dead bugs and microscopic mites whose death would indicate the time of day of the incident.

While the expert is engrossed in his work, our man sits on the front step studying the neighborhood. *Who could have done this?* he thinks to himself. After ninety minutes of examination, the CSI friend is beaming with pride as he holds a sheet in his hand with the results of his investigation. The two sit down over a well-deserved dinner and discuss some answers. "It is obvious," begins the friend, "that a tennis ball has ruptured your window and caused the mess you have. The tennis ball arrived from the northwest at approximately 2:17 p.m. at a thirty-degree trajectory, traveling twenty-three miles per hour. It was seventy-two degrees outside with a relative humidity of 58 percent. The person throwing it was most likely right-handed and was not trying to throw with a lot of intensity— the angle from which the ball hit the window would indicate someone lobbed or tossed the ball."

"So who did it? Why is my window broken?"

The truth is, our CSI expert can't be completely sure. After sputtering through some thoughts like "It most likely is . . ." or "With a high amount of probability it was . . ." we have a lot of data but not a whole lot of answers. It could have been a ball from a sandlot baseball game. It could have been someone playing catch and one throw was errant. It could have been almost anything. "Maybe someone will confess," our CSI expert suggests, finishing the last of his dinner. As the friend gets ready to leave, our homeowner is just as much in the dark as when he started. Lots of facts, but no answers. Waving goodbye to his friend, our man heads to the basement to get some tools to fix the window.

Halfway down the steps, the doorbell rings. Figuring his friend has left something in the house, he heads back to the front door. Standing at the door, however, is a man from down the street. "I'm sorry to bug you so late, I just wanted to explain something to you that I couldn't earlier." Intrigued, our man invites the neighbor in. Stepping through the vestibule, the guest looks right at the broken window. "Sorry for that, and sorry I couldn't let you know earlier. I was walking my dog and a neighborhood kid started playing fetch with him. Well, the kid got a little excited and tossed a long one, and my dog chased it, cutting his leg on the corner of a fence. I took him to the vet to get cleaned up and we didn't get home until now."

Our homeowner smiles—now he understands. He likes things in their proper place, and now that the truth is revealed he feels better. Assuring the neighbor that it is no big deal, our man conveys that it is just good to know the whole story.

"When I came home, I was so confused. It could have been anything, in fact, I have a friend who knows this kind of stuff very well and he gave me a lot of detailed information about what had happened, but I still wasn't satisfied. Now, though, you have explained everything."

"I'm really sorry," the visitor says, "I want to cover the cost of replacing the window."

And so the rest of the conversation continues about what to do from here, but our man has everything he wants. He just wanted to know what happened, and that could not have happened until the doorbell rang. The truth showed up.

7

IN THE FLESH

THE SINGLE LARGEST PROBLEM WITH the truth showing up is that it always shows up where we least expect it. Most skeptics (and if we are honest, even ourselves) would like the truth written across the sky. If only we had some demonstrable proof, some sort of universally accepted evidence of God's presence in this world. It is one thing to say that truth is not made, it shows up; it is an entirely different thing to say where it shows up. And if we are to be consistent we need to acknowledge that if faith lies outside of reason, so does the manner in which it comes to us.

It was the last day of Jesus' life, and he was about to reveal himself in a way that was most intriguing: not a word would be uttered and only one person would witness it. As far as I can tell, that person didn't understand it. Pontius Pilate, the prefect (what we would know as a governor) of the area that included Jerusalem was apparently bothered by the case of Jesus. Prefects were given the order by Rome to maintain the military, collect taxes and essentially keep the peace in the region. Those who didn't keep the peace were replaced (to put it mildly), and Pilate had a history of difficulties keeping the peace.

When Jesus stood in front of Pilate, it was one of the most dramatic moments in all of history (see John 18:28-40). On one side was a very frustrated and beleaguered Roman leader who would rather not be sorting through the religious squabbles of the Jews. On the other we find a beat-up man claiming to be the King of the Jews. This was not the first time Pilate had dealt with a Jewish dreamer claiming to be some sort of promised leader of the Jews, and it would not be the last.

What makes this so dramatic is that Jesus approaches this encounter with a cosmic perspective. This is one of a series of well-calculated steps by Jesus to humble himself to the point of death. He enters the place like no other man. In the strangest sense Pilate is reflexively assisting in his own salvation by washing his hands of the whole affair and allowing Jesus to be condemned to death. Perhaps it is a part of God's own mercy that Pilate is oblivious to it all. Left to what we can observe, we would have no idea of the spiritual implications of what is taking place. The logic is completely paradoxical: Jesus' power absolutely trumps Pilate's, but it is expressed in his own demise. Jesus gains power over sin by submitting himself to death.

As the two enter this arena, Pilate speaks first and asks, "Are you the king of the Jews?" It is his rightful place; Pilate is the judge. The question of his kingship is a starting point for understanding the nature of Jesus' crime. However, Jesus answers with a question, perhaps seeking Pilate's motive—"Is that your own idea or did others talk to you about me?" In Pilate's answer we get a hint of his annoyance at it all: "Am I a Jew?" His manner is terse. Seeking to get things over with, Pilate asks again more directly, "What have you done?" Jesus answers with a cryptic, "My kingdom is not of this world" and goes on to say that when a king is taken captive, the subjects of the kingdom fight for his release. Which prompts the question from Pilate: "Are you a king then?"

Jesus answers "I am," and we can't miss the author's intent in using that phrase. Jews would recognize this phrase as the very name of God (which we will look at in a bit). At the moment, the tension is palpable; Jesus has just upped the ante by identifying himself with God, and Pilate doesn't get it. Jesus then adds that his mission is to speak the truth so that everyone who listens to the truth would listen to him. At this Pilate bites, "What is truth?"

Pause here. Freeze the frame for a minute.

Notice there is no recorded answer to this question. The next thing Pilate does is leave the room. Either he asked it as a throwaway question before leaving or it hung in the air with pregnancy. Both possibilities are poignant, but the silence is most intriguing to me. Is it possible that Jesus does not answer his question because it wasn't sincere? I suppose it is reasonable to assume that since Pilate is clearly annoyed at the whole affair, it is a waste of breath to try to explain what truth is. Pilate had his chance to hear the truth, and now he will hear silence.

As long as we have the pause button on, let's consider another possibility. Is it possible that the question "what is truth?" was a moment of revelation? I can imagine Pilate throwing out the question from a jaded heart. Here is a man who has seen many men lead others in religious rebellion only to be arrested, killed and their followers scatter. "What is truth?" doesn't come from a man who is seeking understanding, it comes from a man who has seen enough pointless religious squabbles and is tired of it all.

Jesus had made a practice throughout the night and up to the moment of Pilate's inquisition to speak very little or remain silent. Perhaps he is fulfilling Isaiah's prophecy:

> He was oppressed and afflicted,
>   yet he did not open his mouth;
> he was led like a lamb to the slaughter,

and as a sheep before her shearers is silent,
so he did not open his mouth. (Isaiah 53:7)

Is it possible that in this silence, Jesus communicates his answer? Instead of telling Pilate about the nature of truth or giving
him a roadmap to discover it for himself, Jesus simply stands in
front of Pilate. You want to know the truth? The truth is standing
in front of you. I am the truth. Jesus is not a bearer of the truth;
he can't help you find the truth; he *is* the truth.

There were a handful of other religious teachers that had sprung
up claiming to be the Messiah, and all of them had claimed to
have access to the truth. All were put to death, and their rebel-
lions were stopped. Most religious leaders of the day were ac-
knowledged by others to have the truth in writing—the Law itself. Mystery cults, soothsayers, prophets, oracles—the ancient
world was not without its sources of truth.

Jesus, however, claimed *to be* the truth. Earlier in the Gospel of
John, when the disciples asked Jesus about the way to God, Jesus
claimed to be "the way and the truth and the life" (John 14:6). In
fact John records several instances when Jesus claimed to be something by invoking the sacred "I am" associated with God himself.
Jesus says, "I am the bread of life" (John 6:35). "I am the light of
the world" (John 8:12; 9:5). He says, "I am the good shepherd"
(John 10:11-14). "I am the resurrection and the life" (John 11:25),
and "I am the true vine" (John 15:1). The emphasis in these passages is on the verb, not the modifier. Jesus is the "I am."

These claims were blasphemous to the Jews because they put
Jesus on par with God. So how ironic it is that Pilate asks what the
truth is and then walks out of the room where the truth is standing. How tragic. The truth showed up, not cryptically written
somewhere or discovered in some corner of the universe. The
truth came to Pilate, and he wasted his chance at finding it. Some

people spend their lives reading in search of it. Others travel, and some submit themselves to years of religious training and devotion. The truth, however, is not hard to find because it is actually finding us.

Let's go back for a moment to the story of the broken window (chap. 6). If you remember, our man had shattered glass on the floor and a hole in the window. He invited his friend over to tell him all that he could about the crime scene. He did an amazing job, allowing the man to account for everything, including the direction, speed and size of the object thrown through the window. However, until the other man arrives at the door and explains why the hole got in the window, we have no certainty about what happened.

This is the condition that we are all in. Everything we see—mountains, lakes, meadows, animals, people—points to the fact that *something* happened to get us here. The problem is simple:

1. We are here. Most of us (with the exception of the most skeptical philosophers) would not doubt this.

2. We are equally as sure that at one point we were not here. There was a time before humans were here, and now we are. There also was a time before our own birth when we were nonexistent.

3. So what happened? No one is sure, but we can be sure that *something* happened.

And scientifically, we can know *how* it was done—even up to a nanosecond before the glass broke, we have facts littered all over the floor, but no truth. Without the critical information of *why it happened*, we are just as empty as when we started. The unanswered why is the hole in the window. The answer is the person at the door. Truth is not discovered, it shows up.

Now there are lots of attempted answers to the why question—from it all being a cycle of birth and rebirth to "all we are is dust

in the wind." Most answers remain on the two-dimensional surface of the plane that we call knowledge. There are many who
hold beliefs that remain tied to the five senses and attempt to
comport with reason. But Christianity becomes warped when it
is pressed into two dimensions because its native environment is
one of depth. The presence of a person as the truth takes the
premise of Christianity out of the two-dimensional arena and
puts it into the three-dimensional expanse of theological space.
Truth exists as a person who comes to us. It changes all the pa-
rameters that we previously had and makes the most casual observer at least admit that there is something radically different
about the truth as a person.

Jesus answers Pilate with presence. He simply stands there in front
of him. What is truth? It is the person of Jesus, and this is consistent
with Old Testament Scripture. The God of the Bible is the God
who is *there*. God simply prefers to be present. While other gods had
great descriptions, God described in the Old Testament is more interested in presence—on showing up and *being* with his people. God
knocks at the door and explains the mess on the floor.

This revelation was often bizarre, jarring and strange. Repeatedly, humans who encounter God in the Old and New Testa-
ments are encouraged to not be fearful and in some instances to
get off the floor. Their fear is understandable. Seeing something
beyond the usual in a dimension that is unfathomable is strange
and stressful. But we have seen there is an intimate connection
between what is true and what is strange. Our minds tend to
throw out the things that we aren't able to flatten, so maybe these
things that are so strange are the most real.

Early in Genesis, God's encounter with Abraham begins a relationship with a family in the Middle East. God promises child-
less Abraham that he will have a son who will eventually father a
nation. Abraham could have simply received this promise—story

complete. But God later enters into a covenant with Abraham. We meet Isaac, Abraham's son, and the assurance from God that "I will be with you" (Genesis 26:3), which extends to Isaac's son Jacob (Genesis 31:3, 12). Hundreds of years later God reveals himself to Moses in the midst of a bush that seems to be on fire. Again, God assures Moses that he will be protected by God's divine presence (Exodus 3:12). And God assures Joshua, Moses' protégé, that God will be with him (Joshua 1:5). Gideon, David and Solomon receive the same promise (Judges 6:16; 1 Kings 11:38). In Isaiah 43 the entire people of Israel can lay claim to this promise. When the people of God go through trials, they can expect the presence of God to guide them through it.

> When you pass through the waters,
> I will be with you;
> and when you pass through the rivers,
> they will not sweep over you.
> When you walk through the fire,
> you will not be burned;
> the flames will not set you ablaze. (Isaiah 43:2)

There is something calming and reassuring about this phrase— *I will be with you*—that transcends the rationalistic debate and arguments for or against the Bible. For me it provides a calm reassurance of the presence of God. Where other religions may talk about the way to God, the Old Testament says God shows up on our doorstep.

More than just showing up, God *reveals* who he is. God is not just present but opens up to us and reveals what makes him tick, what makes us want to follow him. In Exodus 3, when Moses is asked to approach the Egyptians, he reluctantly agrees, but among other things he wants to know God's name. To the ancients the name of a deity was serious business—it held the fear and power of the deity and was not to be spoken loosely. The Egyptians had intimidating gods depicted by human and animal forms, and had names like Shu (a crocodile), Horus (a falcon), Atum (a serpent), Apis (a bull). They had an identity that commanded respect. Their forms represented why they were to be feared. So it is likely that Moses wants a divine name that will inspire reverence or fear, or both, when he talks to the Egyptians. At the very least Moses wants to know who this God is. Perhaps Pilate was being sarcastic when addressing Jesus, but Moses was earnest—who are you?

So what name does God give? Historian Thomas Cahill calls it the greatest mystery of the Bible. God simply answers *I AM*.

> Moses said to God, "Suppose I go to the Israelites and say to them, 'The God of your fathers has sent me to you,' and they ask me, 'What is his name?' Then what shall I tell them?"
>
> God said to Moses, "I am who I am. This is what you are to say to the Israelites: 'I AM has sent me to you.' "
>
> God also said to Moses, "Say to the Israelites, 'The LORD, the God of your fathers—the God of Abraham, the God of Isaac and the God of Jacob—has sent me to you.' This is my name forever, the name by which I am to be remembered from generation to generation." (Exodus 3:13-15)

An interesting choice of words. We get no hint of how the Lord *functions* (sun god, storm god, fertility god). Neither do we know why he should be revered. He simply is. God is there. There have been many guesses about what *I AM* means. Cahill summarizes three outstanding possibilities:

1. *I am who I am*—The name implies totality: "I am he who causes (things) to be, . . . I am the Creator."

2. *I am who I am*—"You cannot control me by invoking my name"; in short, "buzz off."

3. *I will be there with you*—This "emphasizes God's continuing presence in his creation, his being there with us."[1]

In some ways, I resonate with the first explanation. Perhaps God is saying, "I am above your categories; I simply *am.*" On deeper reflection, what would mean more to Moses and the Jews at this point than the divine presence and the revelation that God desires to be among them? Rather than some kind of explanatory or functional term that describes who he is, the answer is in verb form—the God who is and does, and will be and will do. He is there. Yahweh is not described by words, but a state of being— *among* us. He shows up. He chooses presence over explanation. Relationship versus description. *I am.*

As the story continues, God kicks in the door and rescues his bride, the nation of Israel, from the Egyptians. Next, he helps them escape into the desert through the Red Sea. Once they have escaped, God meets them and enters into a covenant with them on Mount Sinai. While this is alien to us, it carries the weight of intimacy for the ancient Jews. God reveals more of himself by giving the Israelites a set of laws to live by.

When we think of law, we tend to think of dos and don'ts— someone defining the limits of acceptable behavior. Not very intimate. When I think of laws and rules, I am reminded of traveling to my grandmother's for Christmas; the entire hour-long ride was a recounting of the right and wrong things to do while at her house.

• Say hello to everyone.

• Give your grandmother a hug.

• Don't hover around the snack area. Take one thing and then go do something.

• Don't ask for more than one soda.

• Say thank you no matter what you get for a present.

My brother Chuck would roll his eyes and say, "Okay, we get
it!" My dad would yell at him and my mother would start over
again. It was not the best way to visit family. I was so focused on
what I should *not* do that I was never really visiting with them.

This is not the way that observant Jews would have regarded
God's law. The law brought order to an often chaotic world. The
fact that God would care enough to give them the law in a time
when chaos and lawlessness was abundant revealed that God cared
about the lives of his people.

We really can't understand what something like the law meant
to the Jews. It was more than just giving out rules; God was showing a little more of himself. The giving of the law at Sinai revealed
the personality of the lawgiver.[2] By delivering the law to the Jews,
God was inviting them to live in rhythm with him. The law is
more than just a prescription of how to act; it's a revelation of
God's presence in the lives of his people. So much of the law dem-
onstrates his presence, the fact that he is the one who is there.
Again, he is the *I am.*

In Leviticus 11:45, God declares: "I am the LORD who brought
you up out of Egypt to be your God; therefore be holy, because I
am holy." When we hear "be holy" we should not think
"Straighten up and stop sinning" but rather "Draw close to me as
I draw close to you. Be like me. Learn from me." The holiness of
God called men and women to demonstrate their own personal
holiness. This shared holiness was a source of connection with
God, an intimacy and presence. Make yourselves different from
everyone else—just like I am different from anything else. Set
yourselves apart for me; be as I am. As a father teaches his son, the
law teaches us how to be like God. So when we see commands in
Leviticus about circumcision, the length of beards, the mixture of
fibers in clothing and such, we are aware of a God who is present
in daily matters, a Father who is there.

Through the law, which reveals the heart of God, we learn that God is truthful—say what you mean and mean what you say; don't lie; and keep your hands off other people's property. God cares about family: parents are to be honored, husbands and wives are to stay together, don't murder people. We learn from the law that God loves his people—he provides all we need and helps the widow, the orphan and the foreigner. As a community of people, look out for each other, worship together, celebrate God's goodness at growing time and harvest. Take a day off each week and be thankful for what you have. Set aside a day each year to forgive people, come to God in confession, and make things right with enemies. Ultimately the law helps us see a holy God who is eager to forgive and bless many generations. His law reveals himself—something endearing and intimate to the people of Israel (and ultimately the world). This is not just a contract with stipulations; the law is a presentation of the *person* of God.

I used to wonder why the Psalms talked so much about loving the law. When I looked at the Old Testament code, I wondered what made the psalmists overflow with delight in something that seemed so . . . *legal?*

Blessed is the man
>who does not walk in the counsel of the wicked
or stand in the way of sinners
>or sit in the seat of mockers.
But his delight is in the law of the LORD,
>and on his law he meditates day and night. (Psalm 1:1-2)

The law of the LORD is perfect,
>reviving the soul.
The statutes of the LORD are trustworthy,
>making wise the simple. (Psalm 19:7)

Blessed is the man you discipline, O LORD,
   the man you teach from your law. (Psalm 94:12)

I will praise you with an upright heart
   as I learn your righteous laws. (Psalm 119:7)

The answer is that the Jews saw in this law the presence of
God. It was not a flat document that acted as a whip to get people
in line. It was more than a prescription for behavior; it was a revelation of the wholly Other. There is a rich history of not just
God's dealing with the Jews in Egypt but the fact that God took
his bride away to Mount Sinai and married her there. The law is
that intimate.

Sadly, this understanding of the revelation of God through the
law was lost. Following God became a study of how to procure
God's favor. The Israelites sought to make the law into a hoop
through which they must jump to get back on God's good side.
To be fair, perhaps it was the knee-jerk reaction of religious leaders who warned of God's wrath, as the tone in Israel became one
of continual repentance when king after king went astray.[3] Perhaps it came from the sting of ignoring the warnings of prophets
and priests, which led to exile that empowered the religious leaders to prescribe the law as a road back to God's blessing. Getting
serious with the law—building a fence around Torah—might
cause God to notice their devoutness and seek to restore them to
a place of prominence among the nations again. Instead of draw-
ing near to *I am*, Israel tried harder and harder to fulfill a legal
code that continued to become "hairsplittingly bizarre."[4] As a
result, the law concerning the sabbath, which was meant to convey the rhythm of God, now became the subject of legal minu-
tiae. The three-dimensional revelation of the person of God was
becoming a two-dimensional legal and ritual code.[5]

Just listen to God's response to Israel:

"The multitude of your sacrifices—
    what are they to me?" says the LORD.
"I have more than enough of burnt offerings,
    of rams and the fat of fattened animals;
I have no pleasure
    in the blood of bulls and lambs and goats.
When you come to appear before me
    who has asked this of you,
        this trampling of my courts?
Stop bringing meaningless offerings!
    Your incense is detestable to me.
New Moons, Sabbaths and convocations—
    I cannot bear your evil assemblies.
Your New Moon festivals and your appointed feasts
    my soul hates.
They have become a burden to me;
    I am weary of bearing them." (Isaiah 1:11-14)

The Jews were trying to figure out how to placate God through religious ritual—through observing the rituals, offerings and festivals. A few verses later God reminds them that what he wants is for them to drop the rituals and be like God.

Wash and make yourselves clean.
Take your evil deeds
    out of my sight!
Stop doing wrong,
    learn to do right!
Seek justice,
    encourage the oppressed.
Defend the cause of the fatherless,
    plead the case of the widow. (Isaiah 1:16-18)

So just as the law revealed a God who was interested in being present among his people, the prophets begin to reveal a second movement of God that was concerned with reclaiming this sense of intimacy that had been lost. Not only would God reveal who he was, this time he would do it *in the flesh*. The law that was flattened would be given new life in the person of Jesus.

As we know, this plan was not well received. The process of giving depth back to the law was threatening to those who saw their duty as defending the legal code. Jesus was a big obstacle to those who were focused on remaining obedient to a law that now enveloped tradition, because he wanted them to see the heart of the law. In the same way that skeptics scoff at Christians for their lack of evidence, Jesus too was hounded for evidence:

> Then the Jews demanded of him, "What miraculous sign can you show us to prove your authority to do all this?" (John 2:18)

> The Pharisees came and began to question Jesus. To test him, they asked him for a sign from heaven. (Mark 8:11)

> The Pharisees and Sadducees came to Jesus and tested him by asking him to show them a sign from heaven. (Matthew 16:1)

> Others tested him by asking for a sign from heaven. (Luke 11:16)

Flattening things has a long history. These evidences were important to the religious leaders because they existed on the flat plane of religious law. Jesus was coming to them as the law in the flesh. As such, the examples Jesus used and the methods he employed were complete nonsense to the leaders. The religious leaders were in two-dimensional mode, and when Jesus intersected their sphere of influence, it looked a lot like Jesus was trying to abolish the law. It is ironic that the law of God made flesh was accused of wanting to do away with the law.

Jesus responds, "I have not come to abolish the Law or the Prophets . . . but to fulfill them" (Matthew 5:17). The law was delivered to you as a person, you have dissected it, and I am bringing it back to life.

> Woe to you, teachers of the law and Pharisees, you hypocrites! You give a tenth of your spices—mint, dill and cumin. But you have neglected the more important matters of the law—justice, mercy and faithfulness. You should have practiced the latter, without neglecting the former. You blind guides! You strain out a gnat but swallow a camel.
>
> Woe to you, teachers of the law and Pharisees, you hypocrites! You clean the outside of the cup and dish, but inside they are full of greed and self-indulgence. Blind Pharisee! First clean the inside of the cup and dish, and then the outside also will be clean.
>
> Woe to you, teachers of the law and Pharisees, you hypocrites! You are like whitewashed tombs, which look beautiful on the outside but on the inside are full of dead men's bones and everything unclean. In the same way, on the outside you appear to people as righteous but on the inside you are full of hypocrisy and wickedness. (Matthew 23:23-28)

It is clear that Jesus was a literal fulfillment—the flesh of the law, as it were. The very law of God that they were trying to keep was standing in front of them. This process of Word to flesh is intriguing: While we attempt to figure things out, whether theologically or scientifically, the truth shows up in the form of a person. While we are sifting through the shards of glass on the floor, Jesus is waiting patiently at the door.

8

NO STRANGER TO NONSENSE

JUST BE WHO YOU ARE. Some people would benefit from this small maxim in big ways. Let's face it, everyone knows when we are trying to be something we are not. Let me take you to Salem, Massachusetts, on Halloween night in the mid 1990s. I was in school nearby and a few friends had asked if I was interested in visiting the central park of downtown Salem on Halloween night. Apparently witches and warlocks gather there on Halloween to do whatever witches and warlocks do. As a young man who didn't mind talking to people about faith, I looked forward to the opportunity to engage a witch or a warlock in conversation. Maybe I could learn something, or vice versa.

On my way there I remember trying to imagine what a warlock looks like. What sort of image do you conjure up for witches and warlocks? As we arrived it was clear that the town was filled with people who were eager to celebrate Halloween and catch a glimpse of a witch at the Witch House or go on the Witch Tour. I am sure that if I were hungry I could have had a witch burger with magic potion, a side of Coke and warlock fries. It was pretty commercialized. I was told that on Halloween everyone tries to get some time with a celebrated witch who lives on the main street of Salem. There was a lot of energy that night, and the town was packed. We made our way to the park where the lesser-known witches would hang out, and it was like walking into a junior high dance. Clusters of darkly clad people—some with hats and capes, most with fake fang teeth, occupied different sections of the park in their own little circles.

At one point I was able to strike up a conversation with a young man whom I'll call Roger. He had tried, as the others did, to present himself as unpredictable and dangerous, but it was clear that Roger was a pretty average warlock, nothing especially frightening about him. I asked him where he became a warlock and what it means. He began to mumble something about an amulet he was wearing around his neck, a five-pointed star within a circle. He called it a pentagram and described himself as a Wiccan, and told me he worships Satan.

Wiccans don't worship Satan, for the record. This was my clue that he was confused and just trying to unnerve me; it didn't work. Imagine Napoleon Dynamite in a cape with fake fangs and a five-pointed star around his neck, trying to convince you that he is a real menace to good people everywhere. Well, I couldn't help myself. I asked to look more closely at his amulet and noticed that the five pointed star was upright within the circle. I said, "Roger, this is a pentacle, not a pentagram; you have an ancient symbol that has been used by all kinds of people throughout history—Babylonians, Greeks, Wiccans—but they don't worship Satan with it. It represents the five elements."

He just looked at me confused for a moment. I continued, "A pentagram is an upside-down star that outlines a goat with his two horns that represents the inversion of the natural order and is often used by Satanists to symbolize their ideas, but this isn't a pentagram." It was clear that Roger was posing as something that he wasn't. He stepped into me as if to confide something and said, "Look, I'm just a computer programmer who comes out here each year because the girls are hot."

And there it is—the truth! We both had a furtive laugh, and I thanked him for his honesty. We had a really good conversation after that about faith, God and the universe. No great conversions were made that night, but things really took off when Roger was true to himself. He was no Satanist; he was a normal young man who liked to hang out with cute witches on Halloween. We can work on his decision-making later. For right now one thing is clear, Roger was a bad actor and an even worse Satanist.

It's not easy to like a poser. We can learn something from this as people of faith. Christianity gets awkward when it tries to cloak itself in something that it is not. In an effort to appear more rational and logical, Christianity has gotten away from its roots. Perhaps we shouldn't worry so much about how it all appears. Christianity is a glaringly odd belief system that does not fit in with scientific empiricism. Are we okay as people of faith to ignore the pressure to be reasonable, to make sense? Who do we look to as a model for this?

We should go back to the beginning. When the Christian faith was new is perhaps when it was at its most laughable. The early church was born into a world dominated by Greek thought.

The Greek culture was a very impressive and influential force that continues to impact even our modern understandings of astrophysics, architecture, rhetoric and mathematics, to name a few. As an example, Democritus lived in the fifth century B.C. and developed the basis for modern atomic theory. He gave us the word *atom*, theorized that the world was composed of them and that they gave specific substances their properties. Pythagoras and Euclid developed an advanced system of geometry we still study today. Hesiod's *Theogony* chronicled Greek mythology and is still studied by students of the classics. Sophocles crafted the tragedy. Hippocrates gave us a medical ethical system we use today. And Aristotle had a part in the development of the scientific method.

We can't forget Socrates and Plato; historian William Barrett regards the last two thousand years of philosophy as a footnote to their work.[1] What is staggering is that these are just several of the dozens of influential thinkers that emerged from ancient Greece who still have an impact on us today. If there was ever a sophisticated and intelligent culture that could confront and defeat Christianity, it was Greek culture.

So when the first Christians brought their message to the world, they knew that they were encountering a culture with quite a few road blocks. The smart move would have been to work within the framework of this impressive culture—try to sound smart and philosophical, try to package it in a way that the Greeks could understand and take hold of. It is obvious, though, that the early Christians were intent on relating their experience with the risen Christ regardless of how it played. The early Christians knew that the "Jews demand miraculous signs and Greeks look for wisdom," but they decided that they would proclaim "Christ crucified" (1 Corinthians 1:22-23). They emphasized that God came in the flesh and did mighty works among them—chief among them being the resurrection.

For the Jews the Word of God was tied to the Old Testament idea of God's law being the irrevocable contract between God and Israel delivered on Mount Sinai. Early Christians, most of whom were Jews, believed Jesus is the human form of that revelation of God. He is the fulfillment of God's promises to the people of Israel. This is a poetic, prophetic and provocative theological idea. The Word of God becomes human and walks among us—not just telling but showing us the rhythm of God in the world.

It was provocative for a few reasons. The tie between the Word of God and the law was overlapped by the Hellenistic (Greek) idea of "word" or "logos." In the Socratic world logos was the steering principle behind the universe.[2] In Greek, *logos* means "reason, intent, meaning or purpose."

So it is obvious that John makes a connection to this idea at the beginning of his Gospel. Writing in Greek to an audience of Jews and Greeks, it seems that John is readily translating the idea of Jesus' divinity as the logos to the Greek audience as well as the embodiment of the law to his Jewish audience.

The problem is that what John says next pretty much defeats the purpose of trying to win over the Greeks. The word or logos had a well-defined meaning for the Greeks. Starting in the third century B.C., the Stoics saw logos as material, "a divinity present throughout the universe, the very principle that caused all things."[3] One of Jesus' contemporaries, Philo of Alexandria, continued to refine the idea of logos into a person or entity that was part of God.

Since God was perfect and couldn't have contact with physical matter, the logos acted as an intermediary between matter and spirit. It was uncertain how much Philo really held to the idea of the logos as a distinct person or whether it was more of an abstract idea, but for most Greeks, the spiritual was good, right and noble, while the material was evil and decaying. This strict duality prevented anything physical (like human flesh) from being spiritual, pure or unstained. Logos became an agent that spanned the gap between the spiritual and the material.

John would have known this, and if he wanted to retain a Greek audience he would have softened some of his language about Jesus as the logos of God. This dualism—the hard and fast line drawn between the gods (spirit) and man (flesh)—is deeply rooted in Greek thought. The flesh is completely opposite of anything godlike. In fact, for Socrates the soul was not free within the body, it "view[ed] existence through the bars of a prison." The soul was at home in "the realm of purity, and eternity, and immortality, and unchangeableness" and is at its best when "she has as little as possible to do with the body."[4] The soul is a product of the heavens, and the body is of earth; the two are not compatible. So to the Greeks (and the entire Roman world dominated by the Hellenistic philosophy), it was absurd to think of the divine coming in bodily form.

Was John influenced by any of this? Remember, the incarnation is a logical impossibility to the Greeks. God and humanity are separated because human flesh is incompatible with divinity. I love how in light of that, John's Gospel opens with a pronouncement that Jesus was flesh. Look at it again:

> In the beginning was the Word, and the Word was with God, and the Word was God. . . . The Word became flesh and made his dwelling among us. We have seen his glory, the glory of the One and Only, who came from the Father, full of grace and truth. (John 1:1, 14)

Revolutionary. This is very daring in an age when the wisdom of the Greeks was highly valued. It is puzzling that John linked the logos—something of the substance of God—with flesh. This was a Hellenistic no-no. John's bold break with Greek wisdom reveals his allegiance to something higher than Greek wisdom.

This kind of spirit is evident in the early Christian community, which did not apologize for being so different. The Greeks laughed at the foolishness of Christianity, and the Jews scoffed at its lack of proof. Peter and Paul proclaimed what they had experienced regardless of how ridiculous it sounded. The early Christians held to their faith and the truth of their experience no matter how the ruling authorities and religious and intellectual leaders responded. In Acts we read that the early believers boldly resisted when they were told to cease preaching about Jesus.

Then they called them in again and commanded them not to speak or teach at all in the name of Jesus. But Peter and John replied, "Judge for yourselves whether it is right in God's sight to obey you rather than God. For we cannot help speaking about what we have seen and heard." (Acts 4:18-20)

This commitment to personal experience in the face of opposition is refreshing. Instead of worrying about establishing credibility, the young faith community stayed true to what they had lived through. They proclaimed the resurrected Christ regardless of its seeming irrationality. In Paul's letter to the Corinthians he embraces the ridiculousness of the gospel. With apparent bravado, Paul is saying, "Yeah, that's right, this is nonsense *to you*." His pride in the oddness of the gospel spills over with his questions to the Greeks:

Where is the wise man? Where is the scholar? Where is the philosopher of this age? Has not God made foolish the wisdom of the world? For since in the wisdom of God the world through its wisdom did not know him, God was pleased through the foolishness of what was preached to save those who believe. (1 Corinthians 1:20-21)

Paul reveals two things in these verses. First, it is *foolish*. "Fine, you win. What I believe is absurd. Now let me tell you what happened." Paul was not taking the position that only the rational is real, in fact, the opposite may be true. Paul was an educated man who could have taken great pride in his ability to explain theological and philosophical difficulties. But he does not parade his academic accomplishments; in fact he is surprisingly humble. Note his tone when he addresses the people of Corinth:

When I came to you, brothers, I did not come with eloquence or superior wisdom as I proclaimed to you the testimony about God. For I resolved to know nothing while I was with you except Jesus Christ and him crucified. I came to you in weakness and fear, and with much trembling. My message and my preaching were not with wise and persuasive words, but with a demonstration of the Spirit's power, so that your faith might not rest on men's wisdom, but on God's power. (1 Corinthians 2:1-5)

Contrary to the rationally exacting world of Hellenism, Paul purposefully sidesteps proofs for his arguments and resolves only to relate his personal experience. When Paul speaks of only knowing about Christ and his crucifixion, he is demonstrating the foundation of the truth—the *person* of Jesus. The Greeks saw this as foolishness. The foundation of Paul's theology was the person of Christ, and he knew that human reason was incapable of conveying that.

In Acts 17, though the people of Athens refer to Paul as a "babbler," they give him a chance to speak. Paul rather eloquently and reasonably speaks of their gods and develops a convincing way to insert the story of Christ. Paul argued convincingly, but "when they heard about the resurrection of the dead, some of them sneered, but others said, 'We want to hear you again on this subject'" (vv. 18, 32).

Paul wasn't the first to be sneered at for his irrationality. While Paul had to deal with the questions of the Greeks, Jesus had a different set of questions from the experts in Jewish law. Jesus' teaching was gaining an audience and being validated by the miracles he was performing. The Jewish leaders, scrambling to explain how Jesus could do the things that he did, attributed it to demonic forces. Perhaps they seized on the fact that he spent some of his earlier life in Egypt and inferred that it was by sorcery that he was performing these acts:

Then Jesus entered a house, and again a crowd gathered, so that he and his disciples were not even able to eat. When his family heard about this, they went to take charge of him, for they said, "He is out of his mind." And the teachers of the law who came down from Jerusalem said, "He is possessed by Beelzebub! By the prince of demons he is driving out demons." (Mark 3:20-22)

The Jews answered him, "Aren't we right in saying that you are a Samaritan and demon-possessed?" (John 8:48)

At this the Jews exclaimed, "Now we know that you are demon-possessed! Abraham died and so did the prophets, yet you say that if anyone keeps your word, he will never taste death. Are you greater than our father Abraham? He died, and so did the prophets. Who do you think you are?" (John 8:52-53)

And the teachers of the law who came down from Jerusalem said, "He is possessed by Beelzebub. By the prince of demons he is driving out demons." (Mark 3:22)

The same holds true for Jesus' followers. They were regarded as being possessed, insane—even drunk! At Pentecost, the inception of the church, the Holy Spirit comes among the followers of Jesus and causes quite a scene (see Acts 2). Peter attempts to convince the hearers that they are not drunk. Why? *Because they sounded drunk.*

There were some that were supposing that they were full of wine. Peter flatly denies that they have been drinking and inserts a curious phrase: "It's only nine in the morning!" Could this be Peter's attempt at a little humor? Next Peter quotes from the Old Testament book of Joel. Now think about that for a minute. Peter calms the crowd and assures them that they are not drunk or crazy by quoting from a prophetic vision that is nothing short of apocalyptic. Apparently Peter didn't mind portraying Jesus' followers as fulfilling the prophet's vision of some pretty strange activities. It is clear that whether it is Jewish religious logic or Greek philosophy, Jesus and the early church learned to survive among those who attempted to impose another way of thinking on them. More than surviving, the early church thrived in part by being comfortable in its own skin.

To be balanced, Paul does use convincing logic in the great passages of Romans and elsewhere in his epistles. Acts bears witness to his tireless efforts of trying to persuade the ancient world through reasoning from the Scriptures:

> They arrived at Ephesus, where Paul left Priscilla and Aquila. He himself went into the synagogue and reasoned with the Jews. (Acts 18:19)

> As his custom was, Paul went into the synagogue, and on three Sabbath days he reasoned with them from the Scriptures, explaining and proving that the Christ had to suffer and rise from the dead. "This Jesus I am proclaiming to you is the Christ," he said. Some of the Jews were persuaded and joined Paul and Silas, as did a large number of God-fearing Greeks and not a few prominent women. (Acts 17:2-4)

His use of logic, however, is different from modern usage. You don't get the feeling that Paul is trying to "make sense" of the gospel or convince people that it is worthy of their attention. Paul doesn't use reason to make the gospel more palatable to logicians. The purposes of Paul's great expositional passages are to explain a foreign way of thinking. It is apparent that Paul is okay remaining in a world foreign to reason—things that are not seen versus things that are seen. Paul himself makes this point to the Corinthians:

> We are not trying to commend ourselves to you again, but

are giving you an opportunity to take pride in us, so that
you can answer those who take pride in what is seen rather
than in what is in the heart. If we are out of our mind, it is
for the sake of God; if we are in our right mind, it is for you.
For Christ's love compels us, because we are convinced that
one died for all, and therefore all died. And he died for all,
that those who live should no longer live for themselves but
for him who died for them and was raised again. (2 Corinthians 5:12-15)

In summary, we are oddball dreamers who live in the realm of
faith. Let's face it, for too long we have been bogged down in an
attempt to establish the intellectual legitimacy of the Christian
faith. Has this pursuit taken us from the original mission and
mandate of the church—namely, to proclaim truth rather than
reshape it? We have flattened the beauty of the message to fit in
the court of human reason.

All of these ridiculous stories with "obvious" mythological elements could have been tidied up by an editor. The Bible, however, retains all of its splendor—a strange set of stories that enjoy
their otherworldliness. Time and again, the biblical authors appeal to the authority beyond the senses.

So we fix our eyes not on what is seen, but on what is unseen. For what is seen is temporary, but what is unseen is
eternal. (2 Corinthians 4:18)

By faith we understand that the universe was formed at
God's command, so that what is seen was not made out of
what was visible. (Hebrews 11:3)

I wish we had this kind of confidence. So much of modern
Christianity is self-consciously awkward. We are always seeking
to validate the truth of Christianity, desperately trying to come to

a point of acceptance by mainstream culture. But the first-century believers are great examples of what can happen when we relate the experience we have with God. Agnostics may want proof, and spiritualists may want to deny the universality of the Christian claim, but it is beautiful to imagine Christians who spent less time trying to prove something and more time proclaiming what God is doing in our lives.

Faith operates outside of reason; having faith is decidedly different from other endeavors. It has its own rules, which are curiously hidden from searchers in a hurry to find the truth. The Bible defines faith as being sure of something that we only hope for (Hebrews 11:1). Even in defining things, the Bible can't escape its own curious logic. The Bible uses "being sure" and "hoped for" in the same definition. But hope and certainty are opposites. How can we possibly be certain of anything we merely hope for? The answer is, *we can't.* We either hope for something or are certain of it. If we are certain of it, we *have* it. Or it has us—we can see it, touch it, taste it, sense it—there is no doubt. To hope for something means we have some measure of doubt in ever obtaining it. If there were no doubt about obtaining it, why would we call it hope? When you flick the light switch you don't hope it comes on. When you wake up in the morning you don't hope there is such a thing as gravity. We reserve a word like *hope* for things that have an element of doubt to them.

When my birthday rolls around, I expect birthday presents. I know they are coming, and they will eventually be given to me. This is not hoping—I am waiting. I might say, "I can't wait for my birthday." I certainly wouldn't say, "I hope for my birthday," because I *know* it will come. Now if I ask for a specific present and I don't know whether I will get it, I am no longer waiting but hoping. There is a measure of doubt involved—I don't *know* that I will get it. If someone tells me I am getting a guitar for my birthday, I am merely *waiting* for a guitar. Otherwise, I hope for a guitar.

But biblical faith is different. It is one step beyond hope and one step behind waiting. We have more than hope because of the assurance we have in the gift-giver. I have assurance that I will get the guitar not because I have seen it or been told that I will get one, but because I know the gift-giver is trustworthy. This is how the logic of Scripture is different—it's rooted not in reason but in my relationship to the Giver.

It comes down to this: virtually no one I have had a conversation with about their faith journey has ever admitted they came to faith through arguments. Most people's journey to faith is specific, strange, peculiar—irrational. Augustine heard a child's voice singing "Take up and read" and thought it was God telling him to read the Scriptures. The passage he read led him to faith. Martin Luther came to faith after suffering from depression about his own sinfulness. John Wesley talks about his heart being "strangely warmed." I don't think I know any who were argued into the faith. That is because there is no argument for God. Our faith comes to us in a Person.

Because our faith comes to us in a person and not in a proof-text, there are going to be things that are beyond what we can explain. As people of faith, we need to be okay with what some might call nonsense. Yes, we do believe in a God that has existed for eternity. He has no beginning and no end. This same God formed us out of the dust of the ground and breathed a soul into us. This soul joined seamlessly with the body to create a living being. No other thing created came from the breath of God. Humans are unique.

When we chose to separate from God, he pursued us with a plan of salvation, which includes the Messiah, who came and died for our sins on a cross. This Messiah, God's own Son, the essence of God, became fully human and lived among us in history. The

Messiah, Jesus, was condemned to die (which was part of God's plan) as a substitute for our sins. So now every person who feels the shame of sin can look to Jesus and by faith ask for forgiveness because God's Son took all sin upon himself.

Jesus established the church—a body of Christ-followers who seek to reclaim the world from the forces of darkness. The church looks for Jesus' second coming and the final judgment of all evil. Equipped with the Helper, the Holy Spirit, we take this message into the whole world to see who will respond in faith. Those who do will enter into eternal life and the adventure of redeeming the world with Christ. Those who don't have chosen a life and after-life apart from God—hell.

The Christian message, in all its bizarre glory, comes from across the sea—beyond the horizon. We heard it from someone else who heard it from someone else who heard it from someone else who heard it from the person who saw it all. The only thing different about people of faith is that they choose to believe the testimony handed down to them. We have no explanation for its origin or its ending. The only thing they have is faith, which is absurd, but that's okay. And all the things that come with it: prayer, worship, charity, sacrificial love—all of it too is nonsense. But we have faith because there is something on the other side of the ocean that beckons us. We feel it through faith. For every person we treat with grace, we come to understand grace more. For every person we show mercy, we take part in something divine that is happening in the world. There is something somewhere that makes a whole lot of sense, but only when we step into it.

9

CIRCULAR REASONING

THE FIRST TIME I SAW DOUBLE DUTCH, I had no idea what I was witnessing. Imagine jumping rope on steroids: two people wave two long ropes in circles, each one in different directions, alternating so that when one rope is going down, the other is coming up. Oh, and there is a person or group of people jumping inside these ropes. They don't just jump rope, though; they sing, dance, do somersaults and flips. Forget all the gymnastics; just jumping rope with two alternating ropes requires insane amounts of balance, coordination and daring. I consider myself pretty athletic, so when I saw it, I wanted to try it. How hard could it be?

I shouldn't have asked. The girls holding the ropes tried to be patient as I kept tripping over the ropes. After four or five unsuccessful tries, I asked one of them for some advice. You would have thought that I had asked her the atomic weight of beryllium. She was completely clueless on how to help me. After struggling with a few thoughts, the girl shrugged her shoulders and said something about just having to "feel it."

Not really sure what to do with "feeling it," I applied all my mental abilities to figuring this thing out while another girl jumped. At some point I felt like I had studied enough and was ready to try it again. Slightly bouncing my knees in the rhythm and trying to convince myself that I had this, I ran straight in like a bull charging a combine.

It was all calculation and no feeling. There is something about Double Dutch that you just have to get in order to do it . . . and I didn't get it. You can't think your way into it, you have to know it before you know it.

What I don't understand about Double Dutch, I do understand about faith. "Knowing before you know" is the same principle at work in faith and is why faith and reason are so consistently at odds. Simply put, faith requires acceptance before proof, and reason requires proof before acceptance. Both reason and faith have bouncers telling you to leave what you have at the door. In order to enter reason, you need to trust only in what you see. In order to enter faith, you need to trust in what you cannot see. Reason is linear; faith is circular.

All of the examples of reason and logic that we have been using up to this point have been linear—meaning it travels *upward* and leads us progressively toward something. A bee stings; the sting hurts; when I see a bee in the future I am very cautious about where it puts its stinger. The logic follows a few simple, small steps and leads to a conclusion that works (I don't get stung). You are either smarter or better prepared to encounter your environment or situation the next time.

When people reason together, they take a point and build on it to form a new conclusion. All involved see each other's side and arrive at new ways of thinking. This is reason at its best, having a beginning and ending point.

All too often, however, arguments—clashes of logic—do not work that nicely. Arguments go in circles because people practice circular reasoning; the very thing that someone is trying to prove is being assumed in the person's presentation. Perhaps as a teenager you argued with your parents about music. They may have said, "The music you listen to is noise! You can't even understand what they are saying!" This is sometimes called "begging the question": the conclusion (it's noise!) functions as part of the argument (you can't even understand what they are saying!). This statement of opinion keeps circling back on itself.

This is the sort of complaint made against matters of faith by champions of reason. Faith asks me to believe something before I have the proof of it. The conclusion is stated in the premise. We have to jump in to the objects of faith before we know what we are jumping into.

A great example of this is found in Matthew 9.

> When he had gone indoors, the blind men came to him, and he asked them, "Do you believe that I am able to do this?"
>
> "Yes, Lord," they replied. Then he touched their eyes and said, "According to your faith will it be done to you." (Matthew 9:28-29)

Not all of Jesus' healings involve this kind of question. Sometimes Jesus would heal people regardless of their level of faith. But then there are these kinds of episodes, where Jesus links faith and the power to heal or to work in a supernatural way. Jesus asks the blind men if they believe he can heal them before he does it. Do they have the conclusion in mind before the premise is established?

It is interesting to see the interplay between faith and the ability of Christ to work.

- *When the disciples couldn't drive out a demon . . .*

  > Then the disciples came to Jesus in private and asked, "Why couldn't we drive it out?" He replied, "Because you have so little faith. I tell you the truth, if you have faith as small as a mustard seed, you can say to this moun-

tain, 'Move from here to there' and it will move. Nothing will be impossible for you." (Matthew 17:19-20)

- *When Jesus was asked to heal a little girl . . .*

  Jesus said to Jairus, "Don't be afraid; just believe, and she will be healed." (Luke 8:50)

- *In healing the blind man . . .*

  "Go," said Jesus, "your faith has healed you." Immediately he received his sight and followed Jesus along the road. (Mark 10:52)

- *When a storm arises . . .*

  The disciples went and woke him, saying, "Lord, save us! We're going to drown!" He replied, "You of little faith, why are you so afraid?" Then he got up and rebuked the winds and the waves, and it was completely calm. (Matthew 8:25-26)

- *When Peter was drowning . . .*

  Immediately Jesus reached out his hand and caught him. "You of little faith," he said, "why did you doubt?" (Matthew 14:31)

- *When Jesus was asked to heal a little boy . . .*

  Jesus asked the boy's father, "How long has he been like this?"

  "From childhood," he answered. "It has often thrown him into fire or water to kill him. But if you can do anything, take pity on us and help us."

  "'If you can'?" said Jesus. "Everything is possible for him who believes."

  Immediately the boy's father exclaimed, "I do believe; help me overcome my unbelief!" (Mark 9:21-24)

In this last episode, it would have been just as easy to heal the boy and move on. The boy is obviously affected in a very severe way—so much so that he foams at the mouth and seizes. In the midst of Jesus' diagnosis, you get the idea that the father is growing more and more anxious about getting help for his son. When it looks as if Jesus is correcting him on a theological point (*"If you can?"*), the father is exasperated and says, "I do believe; help me overcome my unbelief!" It sounds like he is saying, "Look, I believe in you, just *do* something!"

But this is no minor theological point for Jesus. Jesus is using the healing as a teaching opportunity. Faith is an essential foundational element for Jesus; he wants us to believe it before we see it. The kind of belief here that Jesus seems to be asking for is not just "the power of positive thinking" but rather a trust in what God will do before he does it. It asks the person to assume that which they are seeking. It is a circular request.

This circularity is found throughout the New Testament and goes beyond healing. When Jesus rose from the dead, he appeared to Thomas and told him, "Because you have seen me, you have believed; blessed are those who have not seen and yet have believed" (John 20:29). Similarly, Paul told the Roman church,

> But not all the Israelites accepted the good news. For Isaiah says, "Lord, who has believed our message?" Consequently, faith comes from hearing the message, and the message is heard through the word of Christ. (Romans 10:16-17)

Now consider Peter's words reminding the early church that trials are proof that they are already receiving the goal of their faith. Notice particularly how the reality of it precedes its evidence:

> These have come so that your faith—of greater worth than gold, which perishes even though refined by fire—may be

proved genuine and may result in praise, glory and honor when Jesus Christ is revealed. Though you have not seen him, you love him; and even though you do not see him now, you believe in him and are filled with an inexpressible and glorious joy, for you are receiving the goal of your faith, the salvation of your souls. (1 Peter 1:7-9)

Finally, note the exasperation that Jesus exhibits when a man wants him to heal his son.

Once more he visited Cana in Galilee, where he had turned the water into wine. And there was a certain royal official whose son lay sick at Capernaum. When this man heard that Jesus had arrived in Galilee from Judea, he went to him and begged him to come and heal his son, who was close to death.

"Unless you people see miraculous signs and wonders," Jesus told him, "you will never believe." (John 4:46-49)

The sense of exasperation that Jesus seems to have felt is because faith is not a "put your quarter in the slot and get your proof" kind of arrangement. We either embrace Christ or we don't. As an act of the will, like the early disciples, we leave our nets and follow Jesus. Trusting a God that you cannot see, hear, taste, smell or feel is not incremental. You cannot try it out to see if it works.

There are plenty of people who like the idea of God mixed into their lives in manageable amounts—enough to *enhance* their lives but not enough to *wreck it*. But faith is not consumer-friendly. It is not like bathwater—dip your feet in and if it is too hot or cold you can adjust the mixture. Faith only makes sense with both feet in.

So perhaps faith is circular so that it is hard to come by. Perhaps its circularity tests us and helps us see the great value of it. We come into faith not by the things we bring to it (our intellect or our will) but by letting go. Maybe faith is circular for no other reason than it is honest about itself. I mean, when you really consider it, all sources of knowing are circular, including science.

THE CIRCULARITY OF SCIENCE

There are two ways that science is circular. The first has already been argued in this book: how do we know that what we see and sense is real? What stands outside our sense perception that "proves" what we are sensing is real and not just what our minds have created? Richard Popkin, an expert on philosophical skepticism, summarizes this idea:

> To judge the appearances that we receive of objects, we would need a judicatory instrument; to verify this instrument, we need a demonstration; to verify the demonstration, an instrument: there we are in a circle.[1]

When you get a speeding ticket, you can go to court asking whether the police officer's radar gun has been calibrated. If it has not been calibrated in the last year, you might have a case. Why? Because not everything that measures is accurate. It is the same way for gas pumps and clocks and so on. The instrument's accuracy is assessed by a device outside the instrument itself. So who calibrates what we, as human beings, profess to know? We set our senses and reason up as the universal source of what is real, but how can we be sure? It is a circular starting point.

But this is old territory. The second (and perhaps more interesting) reason that we have to be suspicious of science as the great mediator of what is true comes from scientists themselves. As humans, they have prejudices and biases—inclinations to view things in certain ways, even when attempting to be impartial.

You see this especially in politics. I have intelligent friends on both sides of the political aisle. One group has a hundred reasons why the president should be impeached; another group has a hundred justifications for the president's actions. People tend to make up their mind about issues and then track down facts to support those opinions.

Ask people about a Supreme Court justice and you might get the twenty-four-hour news enthusiasts excited. Now try asking people about whether a strip mall goes in their back yard and you have a different result. When the outcome is important, people make up their minds about things that affect them and then look for reasons to support it, not vice versa. People have opinions before the facts on the things that they really care about. Those that claim to be open-minded are most likely just apathetic.

Sociology professor and speaker Tony Campolo was speaking at Dartmouth College about the legitimacy of faith. At the conclusion of his talk, a student asked him why an intelligent man like Dr. Campolo would believe in the Bible. Campolo answered that he decided to, "and once having made that decision I built arguments that supported my decision."[2] To which the student replied, "I'm glad you're honest." Slightly annoyed, Campolo turned the table on the student and said, "Before you sit down, let me ask you a question: why *don't* you believe the Bible? Is it because you decided to and have built arguments to support a priori commitments? So it turns out that you and I are a lot more alike than you might think." What Dr. Campolo asserts is that there are no purely objective people that are swayed by evidence to embrace certain worldviews. All orientations, whether religious or scientific, are arrived at through a decision. Since none of us has access to the rock-solid truth on any subject, we are all circular thinkers—we decide on a conclusion and then go on to prove it.

I have great respect for scientists like the late Carl Sagan, who very persuasively argued that the scientist has to be completely objective and let the results dictate the truth of their findings. In fact, Sagan contended that the scientist should expect their body of knowledge to change and adapt. At best "even scientific truth is merely an approximation."[3] Few scientific authors are as humble and open to the possibility that perhaps there is something more than what we know about this world. Even in his debunking the Scriptures he includes a very sincere "but of course, I could be wrong."[4] Nevertheless, given his emphasis on reason as the exclusive path to truth, he contended that people embrace faith because of a deep-seated need to believe.[5] His bias, limited to what the senses make known to us, did not allow him to see any legitimate justification for faith.

Sagan wasn't alone in this bias. Albert Einstein could not conceive of

a God who rewards and punishes his creatures, or has a will of the kind that we experience in ourselves. Neither can I nor would I want to conceive of an individual that survives his physical death; let feeble souls, from fear or absurd egoism, cherish such thoughts. I am satisfied with the mystery of the eternity of life and with the awareness and a glimpse of the marvelous structure of the existing world, together with the devoted striving to comprehend a portion, be it ever so tiny, of the Reason that manifests itself in nature.[6]

Notice that Einstein's conclusion is rooted in an ethic and not empirical truth. Instead of following the truth wherever it leads, Einstein is expressing his rejection of any truth outside of what he has already determined. His genius notwithstanding, Einstein is guilty here of circular thinking.

You don't need to be a scientist to be opinionated, of course. Philosopher Friedrich Nietzsche was the son of a Lutheran minister and was expected to fill his father's shoes when he died. That didn't happen; Nietzsche ultimately formed some contrary ideas to Christianity, defining faith as "not wanting to know what is true."[7] And in his book *Thus Spoke Zarathustra* he rejected the idea of God entirely: "God is a conjecture: but I should like your conjecturing to be bounded by the thinkable."[8] Mark Twain felt that "no God or religion can survive ridicule."[9] Thomas Edison, famous inventor of a thousand different things, had a vigorous distaste for faith:

> I have never seen the slightest scientific proof of the religious ideas of heaven and hell, of future life for individuals, or of a personal God. So far as religion of the day is concerned, it is a [darned] fake. . . . Religion is all bunk.

Consider journalist (and bestselling atheistic author) Christopher Hitchens:

> The only position that leaves me with no cognitive dissonance is atheism. It is not a creed. Death is certain, replacing both the siren-song of Paradise and the dread of Hell. Life on this earth, with all its mystery and beauty and pain, is then to be lived far more intensely: we stumble and get up, we are sad, confident, insecure, feel loneliness and joy and love. There is nothing more; but I want nothing more.[10]

Are we surprised that Hitchens finds nothing that is convincing about faith when he has already stated his bias, saying, "I want nothing more"?

How about the American philosopher Daniel Dennett:

> The kindly God who lovingly fashioned each and every one of us and sprinkled the sky with shining stars for our delight—that God is, like Santa Claus, a myth of childhood, not anything a sane, undeluded adult could literally believe in. That God must either be turned into a symbol for something less concrete or abandoned altogether.[11]

When people make sweeping generalities that lump people into categories of "sane" or "deluded," it is generally a good idea to be suspicious of some sort of internal bias. Just because these few that I have highlighted have come to prominence in the Western tradition of science and philosophy does not mean that they are any less human than you or I. Because of that common humanity, we can say with certainty that the same circularity that I can be accused of (or which I readily admit) can also be the same circularity that seemingly unbiased thinkers are guilty of as well.

So we can lay aside the idea that because someone is a scientist they are not subject to a bias that can lead them off the path of the truth. When we talk about circular logic, as people of faith we should quickly agree that belief is circular. In order to experience it, you need to believe it. It only makes sense once you are in it. This is what makes Christianity so honest. Let's stop denying that belief requires us to accept the truth sight unseen. Even if science is not able to admit that it suffers from the same circularity, as Christians there is something that is so authentic about someone saying that they believe when they have no reason to. Remember, it was Jesus who said that we would be blessed to have believed and never have seen.

10

DIALOGUE

IT WAS A SATURDAY AFTERNOON and I was sitting on the bottom bunk in my college dorm room listening to Travis lose his faith. Travis and I had met through a mutual friend, and I quickly grew to enjoy his fun-loving energy. He had a contagious smile, greeted people with bear hugs and was always up for doing something fun. Travis had a soft side too though; he was the kind of guy who would listen to whatever problems you had and offer great encouragement when you were feeling low. He was someone you took great comfort in knowing because of his kindness and his seemingly strong faith. No one would have guessed that inside he was wavering. And yet here he was in my room, quiet and somber, elbows on his knees, tilted forward in a chair explaining why he was letting go of God.

I remember sitting on my bed with my roommate Marc trying to think of ways that I could argue Travis back to the faith. I wondered out loud if it was something I had done, since I was not the model Christian. Maybe my hypocrisy had pushed Travis to this. Travis assured me that it was nothing that I had done but rather the lack of something happening in *his* life that had caused him to question God's existence. Travis was letting go because he felt like he wasn't really in a relationship with God.

Travis had a problem that many doubt-riddled Christians have. He explained to us that when he came to faith he was sold on the idea of having a relationship with God, but over time never felt like he was experiencing a relationship with anyone. Hearing other people say, "I feel like God is telling me to . . ." or "The Lord is leading me to . . ." became a source of frustration for him. What was especially isolating to Travis was how unaffected the Bible left him. When he read the Scriptures, he saw God speaking and being present in the lives of people, but this wasn't his experience. He never heard God's voice or felt God's presence, and as a result, he was ready to let go.

Travis explained, "I just don't feel what people normally feel in a relationship. When I pray, I talk, but I don't hear anything back. I'm supposed to have a relationship with God, but I really don't *feel* it. I read the Bible, but that's just reading words from a page— how is that a relationship?" While I don't remember the specific words he spoke that day, I haven't forgotten feeling stunned as I listened to him slowly walk back across the line of faith. I had seen people come *to* faith, but I had never seen them *leave* it. Sitting there with him, I felt empty, like something was slipping through my fingers. I felt pressed to do something—*anything*—that would help Travis feel his faith again.

The scary thing was that, as Travis spoke, I completely understood what he was saying. How can a relationship with God really be considered a relationship at all? When I think of a relationship with a friend, I think of taking a road trip or talking late into the night. As the hours tick away, you enjoy the openness that only exists between friends; your conversation reveals fresh insights and new reasons why you enjoy each other's company. Friendship means having inside jokes and memories that you can instantly pull up and share. At the bare minimum you can hear a friend breathe; they are with you—present. It seems like a stretch to talk about a relationship with God in the same way. How does a relationship stay alive when all you can do is read about the other person?

Still, I had to quickly come up with something that might help Travis hold on to his faith. Some thoughts came to mind of what I could say to him:

"God speaks to us through his Word—read your Bible more."

"Maybe it's *how* you're praying. If you're truly quiet, you'll hear his still small voice."

"Sometimes God is quiet for a reason. Maybe he's teaching you something."

Here's an especially good one:

"Is there some unconfessed sin in your life? Maybe God is speaking but you can't hear it because of unconfessed sin."

All these ideas ran through my head, but I didn't say one of them. Any other time I would have expected these ideas to be surefire, but in that moment they were just absurd. The truth is, I didn't know what to say. It was hard to argue with the fact that, on the surface of it, a relationship with God (in the way that we usually think about relationships) strains reason.

And as I thought more about my list of things to say, I was struck with how mathematical it was. I thought I had learned my lesson that God is not a person who operates within my boundaries of logic, but there I was ready to give Travis a solution set that was equivalent to spiritual geometry.

If God spoke to the people in the Bible . . .
A = God spoke to people in the Bible

and we read the Bible (a record of these conversations) . . .
A (God spoke to people in the Bible) + B (We read the Bible)

then we have a relationship with God through the Bible
A (God spoke to people in the Bible) + B (We read the
Bible) = C (We relate to God somehow through the Bible)

Somehow in that moment this rational proof-set wasn't that powerful.

What I was doing was trying to solve a problem for a friend through theological deduction, flattening the dilemma and making it more rational. Just think of the irony: Travis was doubting God because he didn't have any experiences with him that felt authentic. His inability to make sense of it all was causing him to doubt. And here I was having trouble helping him hold on to his faith because of the exact same problem. My inability to make sense of it *for* him was causing me to have doubts as well. These doubts for Travis began with how the Bible made him feel left out. Just what exactly was Travis expecting from Scripture that would make it all "real" for him? For me, this was the starting point of looking at the Bible in a whole new way.

As I thought about Travis, I realized he was making the Bible do something it wasn't meant to do. The Bible is not meant to be our relationship with God. So many Christians who nurse quiet doubts do so because they are faithful Bible readers and think that a conversation with God only comes from the printed page. They take great pains to parse words and analyze syntax to understand how the revelation of God changed the lives of people in Scripture, but they stop there. Other Christians view a relationship with God as a theological bone dig; the more information we can get about the nature of God, the better. Both of these approaches ignore the impact of Scripture on our own lives—particularly how God's revelation to the people in Scripture changes our lives here and now, in this moment. It accomplishes this by influencing the way that we approach life. When I read something from Scripture, it leaves the page and enters into my mind in such a way as to influence the decisions I make as I move through the world. Because of this influential relationship, the sacred text is evident in how I live my life.

This was part of Travis's problem. The Bible is only the starting point for this action. In some ways, Scripture becomes valid when it is practiced, not just read. Travis was looking for the Bible to speak to him when it is more likely that we hear God speak to us when we act out the faith that we read of in the Bible. Travis had forgotten that the Bible is only the starting point for our relationship with God, not the relationship itself.

Imagine your relationship with God as a view from a window. The view reveals what lies beyond; it's three-dimensional, having depth and richness, allowing each person to see different things from different parts of the room. By no means does it give us all the information about what lies beyond, but it gives us a glimpse of it. If the view is our relationship with God, the window is the Bible—built to give us a picture of God that was walled off by sin. We are meant to look *through* the window and see all we can see. Travis was relying on Scripture as the only way to know God, rather than seeking to know God in the details of his own life.

Sadly, most Christians are content to remain faithful Bible-readers, happy to analyze and observe rather than participate in a faith that changes the way that they interact with the world. Some get excited about having a relationship with God but then don't know how to make it personal. The more they read about revelations to other people in the Bible, the more they get hungry for their own, but they don't turn that hunger into a pursuit of Christ. Jesus had a similar problem with the Pharisees—they had studied the Scriptures but missed that they pointed to Jesus:

And the Father who sent me has himself testified concerning me. You have never heard his voice nor seen his form,
nor does his word dwell in you, for you do not believe the
one he sent. You diligently study the Scriptures because you
think that by them you possess eternal life. These are the
Scriptures that testify about me, yet you refuse to come to
me to have life. (John 5:37-40)

We can be very conversant in the Scriptures, but if we miss
Christ in them, we miss what they are really about. They point to
the person of Christ and shows us how Jesus changes the lives of the
people he encounters—including us. Remember, it was Jesus who
came to fulfill (literally overflow) Scripture (Matthew 5:17).

This fulfillment didn't end with his death and resurrection. We
have the idea that the Scriptures are settled and static, that there is
a backward-looking motion as we seek to incorporate Scripture
into our lives. Rather, the Scriptures are alive with the breath of
God and speak of the One who is alive today. When we read the
Scriptures, they point forward in our lives and should affect the
way we move through this world. As we apply Scripture to our
lives a deeper relationship with Jesus develops. We don't just talk
to God, he talks back as that relationship informs the way we
move through the world. This dialogue continually puts us in a
position to rely more deeply on God.

As an example, look at the story of Abraham. Abraham was a
man who had a rich relationship with God. Notice, however, that
you never observe Abraham waking up early and reading his
Bible or devotionals. No, Abraham did not have a set of Scriptures to read every morning or Bible studies to attend, church
groups to grow in or a weekly sermon that challenged him to
have faith in God. He was an insignificant man living in a place
called Ur who most likely worshiped a moon goddess and had

aspirations of living out the normal Chaldean life.[1] But one day he hears a voice calling him to move his whole family about a thousand miles to the land of Canaan.

Now, as a quick side note, you might think, *I just wish I heard a voice from God—I would respond in a heartbeat to a voice! Then I would know I have a relationship with God!* Well, actually, no you wouldn't. Just talk to the people who witnessed the Red Sea parting and then months later questioned the whole thing and melted down their earrings and jewelry in order to worship a different god. Don't think for a second that you are beyond them. We are all fickle sheep. And looking to verify the experience is rational thinking anyhow. However, that is not the turf of faith. Faith's home turf is belief without sight, being sure of what we hope for and certain of what we don't see (Hebrews 11:1).

In reality, Abraham's relationship with God is inaugurated by his obedience, not his ears. This is very important: God doesn't become real to Abraham because he heard a voice. A voice is a very subjective thing, regardless of what century you live in. A voice could be the result of some bad cheese, fasting or, in some cases, psychotropic agents. God becomes real for Abraham not when Abraham hears the voice but when Abraham chooses to move. His obedience becomes a leap of faith, letting go of what he knows to embrace uncertainty. This uncertainty causes us to depend on God's provision, and that dependence is the root of Abraham's relationship. Abraham gets to experience God's presence as he depends on him. We can have the same experience when we give up certainty and make the leap of faith with our lives:

> By faith Abraham, when called to go to a place he would later receive as his inheritance, obeyed and went, even though he did not know where he was going. By faith he made his home in the promised land like a stranger in a for-

eign country; he lived in tents, as did Isaac and Jacob, who were heirs with him of the same promise. For he was looking forward to the city with foundations, whose architect and builder is God. (Hebrews 11:8-10)

In reading about Abraham, we can decide one of two things: (1) we can analyze the text for inspiration, or (2) we can imitate what we observe. We read of God speaking to Abraham, and it is a revelation expressly meant for Abraham, but it is recorded to help us seek our own experience with God. I read of Abraham leaving his home, and that same voice calls me because it is God-breathed (2 Timothy 3:16); it is available to me and able to influence my life as well. So in an act of obedience akin to Abraham's I set out to leave Ur for a place that I know God is calling me to. Whether it is a calling out of an unhealthy relationship or into the city rescue mission, I seek to imitate the things I read in Scripture. This kind of translation from text to life change begins a dialogue in which God responds through the guidance of the Holy Spirit and life circumstances. In short, a relationship develops.

So we should not look at the people of Scripture enviously wishing we had their relationship with God. Are you kidding? They had nothing to go on but a voice that could very easily have been doubted. And for some reason we get the idea that God's voice was commonplace in ancient times. Remember that these occurrences were not daily—try counting up the number of times that God speaks to people in the Old Testament and then divide that by the number of centuries that we are talking about, and you begin to realize that these people had very deep faith. This faith was made real by their obedience. Hebrews sums it up poetically:

All these people were still living by faith when they died. They did not receive the things promised; they only saw them and welcomed them from a distance. And they admit-

ted that they were aliens and strangers on earth. . . . These
were all commended for their faith, yet none of them received what had been promised. God had planned something better for us so that only together with us would they
be made perfect. (Hebrews 11:13, 39-40)

What we want is different. We want what we believe to be easily transferable and provable. It is easier to convince people of a
faith that tracks with reason. But for people like Travis, this kind
of gospel validation winds up being empty without some sort of
personal experience. By making revelation *make sense* we flatten
it, we force it to comply with the boundaries of sense and reason
and it becomes unsatisfying. We analyze rather than internalize;
analysis keeps Scripture at arm's length, while internalizing Scripture leads to relationship.

Philosopher Søren Kierkegaard said that the problem with ana-
lyzed and flattened Scripture is that though it is meant *for* us, it is not
to us—we are not the subjects of it.[2] For us to experience it firsthand
we need (borrowing a phrase from Kierkegaard) to leap from reason
to faith—a leap from observation to participation. We are not content to accumulate knowledge of God in our head, but seek experiences of God through the way we live our lives. We travel from
objective rationalism (which can never be truly achieved anyway) to
participant subjectivism. The Scriptures come alive to us through
the lives that we lead because we make continual leaps of faith.

This leap is a difficult one. Kierkegaard goes to great lengths to
explain that it involves completely leaving behind what we know
and entering into what we do not know. We can't keep one foot
on both sides. We have to be okay with leaving behind the kind
of Bible reading that seeks validation. Like Pharisees hovering
over Jesus looking for proof, we dabble in the idea of a relationship with God to see if something happens. If we are not sold on

the fact that God is real, and we keep looking for signs or symbols, our spiritual lives will quickly dry up. We cannot simultaneously seek proof and verifiability while also embracing an immaterial relationship with God.

Our leap of faith cannot be just intellectual—from doubt to faith—but must also be from observer to participant. The observer looks for reasons in the text while the participant becomes the text. We leave the reason-dominated, two-dimensional realm of the mind and enter into the physical and three-dimensional space of action on God's Word. Our leap of faith is to do what we are inspired by the Holy Spirit to do. I go from reading the inspired Word of God to enacting the Word of God in space and time. My life becomes sacred Scripture in action.

This approach is the very opposite of a logical approach to the Scriptures. If we want to have a relationship with God, we need to move away from analysis of the text, where we run the risk of dissecting (and thus killing) it, and toward an incarnational approach in which the Scriptures are brought to life in us. We step into the same kind of obedience that we see Abraham take part in. As a result we form a new dialectic:

- We can read about how God worked in people's lives long ago.

- Learning from this about God's nature, we imitate the actions of people in Scripture so that we can similarly place our trust in things unseen.

- The result of our actions leads us to new opportunities for dependency on God, and so begins the process over again.

Or if you are still stuck on the formula:

The Bible details ancient people's relationship with God.
A = We learn about God's nature through other people's experience with him

As we imitate their actions in our lives, we see God move in similar ways.

A (We read about people's relationship with God) + B (We imitate their actions)

As circumstances in our lives change because of our actions, we have fresh new ways to depend more on God and we build a relationship of dependence.

A (We read about people's relationship with God) + B (We imitate their actions) = C (We form a relationship with God through our actions)

This creates an ongoing cycle, a dialogue that occurs between God and us. A relationship.

Of course this is consistent with what Scripture teaches us. The Word of God is a person. Revelation is a relationship between God and humans. God is three-dimensional, transcending human knowledge and reason. Not only can we know *about* him through sense and reason, but we can *know* him as he shows up in our lives and is present. Of course, being present means that we invite him into our actions. And so our relationship with God is three-dimensional as well, made evident in the circumstances of our lives. We are rewarded in our faith by how we are led.

If I could speak to Travis today, I would say that perhaps the reason he feels so shut out of a relationship with God is because he is reading someone else's relationship with God. This is not to say that the way Travis felt was wrong; it is what a lot of us feel when we approach God at arm's length. The hunger for more is natural—and maybe even holy. Where it leads is up to us. We can throw it all away or leap in.

I am no spiritual expert; I don't claim to have all the answers for people who feel distant from God. I do know, however, that we have a church full of hurting people who want to feel God but don't. Perhaps the common thread in their dissatisfaction is a linear way of looking at the Scriptures in which they "fuel up" or have a "quiet time" and expect that reading words from a page will provide them with all they need. It's not that having "quiet times" is bad; I have a "quiet time" myself.

I am reminded of a missions trip to Guatemala that I led some students on a few years ago. After having worked hard for several days, we grabbed some rest time at a beach and spent the day swimming. It was so hot we were all out in the water for hours. A college student who we met while on the trip had a great appreciation for "extreme" things. On one of my last trips into the ocean I saw Chris, our college friend, run out into the water. I remember him saying that he couldn't swim, so I kept an eye on him. When he got out too far, he looked like he was struggling, so I tried to pull him in, but by that time both of us were in a riptide and very far from shore.

I prayed so hard for Jesus to help us, since it was clear we were going to be pulled out to sea. As I prayed, I was overcome with the thought that I was all alone with no one to help. There were no lifeguards, no bystanders willing to help, no Coast Guard—no one. Yet in the midst of this, I heard as plain as day in my head: "swim for the pier." I looked to my right and there was a rather long fishing pier about three hundred yards away that we would obviously miss at the current angle we were being pulled out to sea. But I decided to listen, and we swam to the right. Within twenty feet we hit a sandbar and stood in three inches of water. Salvation had been twenty feet away.

Now, this is an extreme example, and I don't mean to convey that we hear from God only when we risk our lives. In fact, there are many who do what I did and lose their lives. The point in the example is that I was dependent on God alone—I had put myself in a position to need him, and for some reason, I survived. It doesn't always happen that way—sometimes people die—but because I leaped and was forced to rely on God more deeply, I gained more than an intellectual knowledge of him.

For someone like Travis, maybe it is something as simple as putting faith into practice. In college we seek God's voice for our career path. Maybe for Travis that meant taking Abraham's story seriously and leaving school to seek God's direction for his life. I am inspired by two college students I know who have currently given up very nice post–high school plans to work in India for a year. They just up and left because they know that God wants them to serve. They are taking the two-dimensional printed page into a three-dimensional, life-changing relationship. It is not pretty; they often miss home, and just like Abraham, they might not see the fruit of their labor this side of the grave. But if you were to ask whether they felt God was real, they would laugh. How could he not seem real to them when he is consistently sustaining them?

In less dramatic fashion, we all have ways that we can make a leap of faith in our own lives when, in obedience, we seek to actualize the text in our lives. The more we depend on God, the more we need to depend on him. The more we need to depend on him, the more we hear from him. The more we hear from God, the more we will see the view that God intended.

I want to be very clear here. It may sound like I am saying the Bible is not as important as the experience we have with God. That is not the case. The whole reason the stories are recorded in Scripture is so that we can have a relationship with God. We are meant to have a relationship with *God,* not a relationship with the stories of other people's relationships with him. We read the Scriptures, God's principal revelation to us, so that we can have a relationship congruent with the biblical witness. Over time we actually become *more* devoted to Scripture because we are allow-

ing it to shape our lives. The Bible becomes a conduit for the living God to speak to us through its pages. When that leads to actions in our lives that allow us to hear from God, we are no longer
keeping the Scriptures at arm's length. Instead of being inspired
by God's actions in others' lives, we experience him at work in
our lives.

II

DISCONTENT

I JUST CAN'T STATE IT ENOUGH that "making sense" or forming reason is a manipulative process. One way to think of it is to imagine how we build houses. Now, I am not an expert at construction, but, keeping things simple, it involves a few steps:

1. Dig a hole in the earth, a big one.

2. Crush rocks and limestone and make cement to form a foundation.

3. Cut down and strip trees into dried planks (2 x 4s) that serve as the skeleton for the structure. Melt certain kinds of rocks and form them into small shards (nails) for securing the planks together.

4. Squeeze petroleum from the earth to create plastic tubes to bring water into and out of the house (pipes). Melt other kinds of rocks to create long strings of metal (wires) and encase them in plastic to conduct electricity.

5. Melt other kinds of rocks into sheets of glass (windows) and put the sheets at intervals around the structure to see out of the house. Use the same kind of melted rocks to create glass fibers (fiberglass) to insulate the house.

6. Mix petroleum with pebbles to make shingles so the house is waterproof.

7. Create polymers out of petroleum products squeezed from the earth to create siding that looks nice.

Okay, so I probably wouldn't get a job as an architect or engineer, but essentially these are the steps to building a home. We don't think of all the processes involved (extracting oil to make pipes and such). We think it all came from Home Depot—like it just fell from the sky.

What we have really done when we build a house is subdue the world around us. We have changed the environment by chopping down trees, mining the earth and drilling for oil. This angers some environmentalists because they see things inverted: the earth is not here for us, we are here for the earth. From this perspective not only have we changed the environment by cutting down trees and so forth, but we have changed people's minds by making it okay to bend and shape our world to our idea of what a home should be. We take it for granted that a home is a wooden box with shingles on top and indoor plumbing and electricity rather than a cave and a campfire. What we expect to live in has been shaped by civilization. So regardless of whether this is correct or incorrect (with all apologies to the environmentalists), it stands that not only have we subdued the environment in building a house, we have also subdued human thinking about what constitutes a house.

The same is true about our discussion of sense and reason. We will get into it more later, but essentially we have erected a dwelling that is impressive and very helpful, but somewhere along the way we lost sight of what we have submitted to in the process. Rationalism has clear-cut the forests of questions, of the soul, of wonder and of worship, and formed these raw materials into a dwelling that has convinced us we can know everything by employing reason. Not only has it changed the environment, it has changed us as well. We assume that we can perceive all reality. Not only can we know all there is, but if humans can't perceive it, it isn't real. The unspoken assumption of human reason has accomplished two things: it has subdued not just the environment it inhabits but the way that we think about what is true.

Sigmund Freud wrote very convincingly on the subject of submission in his book *Civilization and Its Discontents*. Now, I am not a big Freud fan (I think he could have benefited from a little extra therapy himself), but some of his observations of human nature are profound. Freud thought civilization is directly related to our ability to dominate and subdue.

In his book, Freud begins before civilization with humans in an interconnected web with animals. It is a rather nasty place; death and chaos are continual realities. Certain species feed off of humans and threaten their existence, and other species are human prey. Some environmentalists would like to return to an existence like this, where humans are reinserted into the web of interconnectedness. I vote no. I sort of like the fact that I don't have to make sure that lions aren't eyeing my children for dinner. And I like the fact that my door has a lock on it to keep aggressive individuals from coming and taking my breakfast. Yes, civilization has afforded us a lot of creature comforts like indoor plumbing, warm beds and door locks.

This is a very basic definition of civilization: the ability of humans to bend the natural environment to their own needs and desires. Freud would say that wish fulfillment enabled humans to bend the environment to suit civilization's needs. In other words, humans wanted to sleep in warm beds in a climate-controlled house rather than shiver in a damp cave. So far this sounds good.

Because of our desire to have wishes fulfilled (eating on a daily schedule, freedom from predatory danger, a dry place when it rains), humans have taken themselves outside of the web of interconnectedness and its related consequences. For example, because we live in houses, drive cars and order hoagies from the deli, we no longer have to individually slay beasts to have coats in the winter, walk miles for food or form hunting parties to get meat. It is one of the great human accomplishments to have removed ourselves from an interconnected environment and have a deli counter. Being in the web of interdependence is chaotic and fraught with uncertainty. Civilization, on the other hand, is much more predictable and comfortable.

Reason has operated in a similar manner. In a world of complexity and uncertainty, human reason has lifted itself out of the jungle of mystery and sought to impose its order on the world. Scientific progress enables us to become independent of anything beyond ourselves so that our questions can be answered with certainty. It is a process of domination similar to Freud's civilizing construct. In creating civilization, seeds are planted by the acre, thousands of cows are milked and pigs slaughtered as civilization bends and shapes its environment to suit its needs. Similarly, rationalism has cut the universe in half and permits as true only those things that follow the patterns we observe, which we call "natural law." Anything beyond this, the "supernatural," is relegated to fairy tale and myth, which are not worthy of being true.

Remember, for Freud the creation of civilization involves the first step of subduing the environment, but step two is subduing each other. In the case of rationalism, the first step has been to create an antisupernatural bias, and the second step is to make others submit to it. Submissiveness is not a natural human trait, however. Just as humans had to learn the art of bending trees into houses, they had to learn to bend other humans to their will. Through brute force or more subtle means of religious, sexual or economic power, humans found ways to subdue other humans to achieve their purposes. As part of this process, we have submitted to rationalism, conceding that some things are too wonderful to be true.

We need to be wary of these two directives—conquering the environment and conquering each other—that ensure civilization. Not only does reason assault faith by claiming that all truth comes through the senses, it also assaults our approach to and trust in the Scriptures. For the last five hundred years scholasticism has turned Scripture study into an academic affair that eventually denied the Scriptures of their power. As people who believe in the personal God, we need to be continually renewed by our fresh experiences with God, not by a sense of accomplishment in parsing the biblical text. We are transformed not by descriptive truths but relational ones. Relational truths are fueled by our relationship with God, not by the power of our reason.

In Freud's theory not everyone complies. Some people are discontented with society and want to fulfill their own wishes with no regard to the established structures of civilization. Take thieves for example: instead of following the prescribed route of creating wealth and purchasing things to satisfy their needs and desires, they take from others. They operate outside the established order; they are in conflict with progress and civilization because they think about themselves rather than the group. We have laws against those people. We imprison those who stand in the way of progress and are not good citizens. The individual can be the greatest enemy of civilization.

Civilization's discontents are unable to function within its limits. Some deep, unmet drive makes discontents fulfill legitimate desires (like love, acceptance and even food) in illegitimate ways. They willfully violate the laws of civilization and take food or money because they see no other way to meet a basic need. Yes, some are psychopaths who want to hurt or destroy others, but many have the same desires as you and I; they just lack the resources or the restraint we have in conforming to society.

Others, though, have fundamental problems with the way civilization works. These are legitimate discontents who, because of some deeper sense of righteousness or justice, cannot allow themselves to become a part of society (either fully or in part). Some discontents, for example, refuse to pay taxes. Our own colonial history had many of these rebels at the start of the Revolutionary War. Not being able to bear the burden of taxation without some form of governmental representation, our forebears rebelled and gave birth to America.

In our own day many people groups are discontent with oppressive and abusive regimes. They long to be free and are tired of submitting to the brutal forces that continue to keep them in chains. Freedom movements are alive and well in Cambodia, China, Afghanistan and North Korea. The forceful regimes are led by ideologies that rob the people they lead in order to remain in power. And they have little regard for the people under them.

Christians are the discontents within the structure of rationalism. We will not allow bestselling works that conclude that faith is nonsense to rob people of their right to think beyond the confines of rationalism. We seek to put logic in its proper place, but not the highest place.

This is not new territory, by the way. Followers of Christ have always been on the outside of the establishment intellectually. Because Christians don't submit to the world and its ideas, we are motivated by things that often oppose the culture at large. Christians are blessed when they are poor or mourning or persecuted. The meek are the great heirs of this world. The hungry are fed, the thirsty are quenched and so on. Christians are an anomaly because they thrive in the face of insult, show mercy to those that hate them and make peace with enemies. Christians don't fit the norm of fallen humanity.

Authentic belief in Christ and dedication to following the way of Jesus leads to a life that looks remarkably different from those who do not follow Jesus. Christians should be all right with living in opposition to the supremacy of reason. This may be why followers of Christ have the reputation for being anti-intellectual. (But, again, we do not reject reason, only its supremacy.) Obviously, Christians are rational creatures—we use logic to navigate the world, and we develop technologies that assist and sometimes save our lives. People of faith should not rebel against reason. We should rebel against the placement of reason as the sole determinant of what is true.

As far as being discontents, Christians should be mindful of the limits of reason as we have discussed in this book. This does not mean that Christians should continually point out the gaps in scientific research. When Christians try to fill the gaps with God, it ultimately backfires. When those gaps are filled in by further scientific research, it seems as if God has been dethroned from a spot where he never set up court. The emphasis, rather, should be on the limits of human understanding, such as the hollowness of observing patterns in the universe but not getting any closer to its purpose. It is great that we can detect water on Mars or observe planets outside the solar system, but the big questions like "Why are they there?" remain unanswered.

So, as a discontent, I push for something deeper and more rewarding. I don't want to know the surface of things, I want to know the depths—the mind of God. It is important as a discontent of rationalism to draw that distinction. Somehow, in the midst of our sound-byte-driven world, people are being convinced that science has the answers to why all this is around us.

Bestselling books conclude that reason is the best answer for all our questions, thus dethroning God. This is our focal point as discontents. Science has a lot of compelling and fascinating answers, but not to the ultimate questions, which can be answered only by a person.

12

ECHOES OF GOD

"WHAT WOULD HAPPEN IF I LET GO OF THIS PENCIL?"

"It would drop to the floor," is always the response.

"Of course it would, because gravity is a law of nature that you can't change. Regardless of the way you feel, it will always drop to the floor."

This was one of the ways that I would talk with college students about the flimsiness of postmodernity. At the time I never even imagined how this argument could be turned inside out and used against the faith I was proclaiming.

I went to college in the early 1990s, when postmodernism had begun to enter the mainstream. Young people were being branded as having abandoned absolutes. They were drifting from the concepts of right and wrong. Christian speakers and authors were assembling armies to combat moral relativism. Being a part of a campus evangelistic ministry, we saw it as our duty to convince people that moral relativism was dangerous. There are absolute rights and wrongs, and it doesn't matter what you think or feel, they are right and wrong every time.

The clinching argument for these absolute laws was the pencil experiment. We would recite, "Just as there are physical laws that govern the universe, so there are spiritual laws that govern our relationship with God." When we drop a pencil, it always falls to the floor. Gravity is a law, a force that exists in the world regardless of our personal feelings and ideas.

The problem with this analogy is that it can be used *against* Christianity as well. Using this idea we could attack the very core of Christianity: When a person dies, the corpse never reanimates. This happens every time without exception. There is a problem with trying to employ logic to argue for something that extends beyond the borders of logic. Logic can only go so far in a religion that has so many fantastic elements to it.

But isn't it odd that God, who presumably gifted us with logic, doesn't want us to use it as a means to discover what he has to offer? Doesn't it seem like a waste of an enormous ability? What do we do with logic when so much of Christianity lies outside of its boundaries?

The bigger question in a book that deals with irrational faith is, how can we say anything intelligible about faith without reason? If truth is truly irrational, then why am I attempting to convey this in a rational manner? In fact, how can we say anything about faith if at its core it's irrational? In order to convey the ideas that I am arguing for, reason must take center stage. So we cannot be rational anarchists. There is a time and place for logic and reason—even human-centered and sense-based logic and reason.

The force of this point gains momentum when we consider some of the biblical texts that employ reason. It seems that God wants us to approach him at times with reason—figuring things out with the rational mind he gave us. Though "the fool says in his heart, 'There is no God,'" God looks from heaven "to see if there are any who understand, any who seek God" (Psalm 14:1-2). Jeremiah puts it poetically:

"Then you will call upon me and come and pray to me, and I will listen to you. You will seek me and find me when you seek me with all your heart. I will be found by you," declares the LORD, "and will bring you back from captivity." (Jeremiah 29:12-14)

Isaiah portrays God as wanting to reason with us:

"Come now, let us reason together,"
   says the LORD.
"Though your sins are like scarlet,
   they shall be as white as snow;
though they are red as crimson,
   they shall be like wool." (Isaiah 1:18)

Now obviously a God who tasks his creation with finding him must have enabled the selfsame creation with the abilities to find him. In short, reason must be a vehicle through which we are able to find God. Isaiah even portrays God wanting us to "reason together," which has the weight of arguing together in an effort to make a case and "prove" something.[1]

In the New Testament we similarly find the importance of using one's reasoning faculties. Acts repeatedly details that "as was his custom" Paul would travel to different synagogues and *reason* with the Jews or the Greeks about Jesus the Messiah. He didn't relate his personal conviction or merely discuss his relationship with the risen Jesus.

Many of his preaching ventures left mixed results, with many concluding that he was speaking pure nonsense. At Athens some men just sneered and walked away. Paul was used to this kind of reception. When he tried persuading King Agrippa and the Roman procurator Festus, Festus exasperatedly responded, "Your great learning is driving you insane!" Paul confidently exclaimed, "I am not insane!" and asserted, "What I say is true and reasonable" (Acts 26:24-25).

When Festus asserts that Paul is being driven mad by all of his astute learning, he is not just saying that Paul is crazy. In this specific instance in Acts, Paul's great learning is equated with someone who has become drunk. Sounds familiar—remember Pentecost? Paul responds by saying that what he is saying is true and reasonable. In other words, he is *sober*. The word used goes to the heart of the Greek idea of someone who is reasonable—serene, quiet and at peace, not stirred up by possession or insanity. Paul, if you will, trumps Agrippa by saying that he is not mad. In fact he is like those paragons of Greek logic; he is stilled by a sober mind focused on the logic of God.

In Paul's theology there is plenty of room for the logic of God. In 1 Corinthians Paul describes a child's thinking process and then says that when we grow up we drop our childish ways and adopt mature reasoning. Paul seems to be arguing against a relativistic logic inspired by relationships. He says that when we grow up we put away fairy tales and childish logic, and embrace things the way they really are. In the same way, Paul argues, we ought to put aside foolish ideas that are out of step with the logic of God (1 Corinthians 13:11).

Paul isn't the only one who uses logic in this way. Peter speaks of being ready to offer an answer to everyone who asks about the reasons we have for holding to the faith. James speaks of the wisdom from above as being *peaceful*, *gentle* and *reasonable* (James 3:17 NASB). Even in the book of Jude we read that those who are hostile to the faith are like "unreasoning animals" (Jude 10).

The method and message of Christ is reasonable as well. Jesus and the disciples proclaimed the coming kingdom of God. And how do we relate a message if it is not at least intelligible? How do people receive it and understand it if it is not reasonable? Not only is it related through a language, which has rules of its own, but it fits into the larger framework of religious thought (i.e.,

Judaism). It is apparent that Jesus had at least some regard for logic in the way he continually refuted the religious elite with well-crafted arguments.

At the beginning of Jesus' ministry some religious leaders had serious objections to what Jesus was doing on the sabbath. Because they believed that disregard for the sabbath was one of the major reasons for Israel's downfall as a nation, observance of the sabbath was strictly enforced. But they had missed the bigger picture and settled for arcane rules about how to observe the sabbath. They clashed with Jesus on one sabbath when he was about to heal a man with a withered hand. As the religious leaders watch him, Jesus asks, "Is it lawful to heal on the Sabbath?" He then goes on the ask, "If any of you has a sheep and it falls into a pit on the Sabbath, will you not take hold of it and lift it out?" (Matthew 12:10-12). Jesus is presenting a logical argument to reveal that pulling a sheep out of a pit is not work but an act of mercy. In the same manner, his act of healing is an act of mercy.

On another occasion Jesus is approached by what Luke calls "spies," who were eager to argue Jesus into a corner and expose faults in his teaching. Luke says that they hoped to verbally entrap Jesus so they could arrest him. The first subject that they bring up is whether a Jew should pay taxes to Caesar. So Jesus has someone bring him a coin and points to the image of Caeser on the coin saying, "Give to Caesar what is Caesar's, and to God what is God's." Then they asked him about marriage and the resurrection, because the Sadducees didn't believe in the resurrection. Jesus answers that marriage relationships are superseded by the arrangements in heaven. Then he attacks their position on the afterlife. Referring to Exodus, Jesus recalls that in speaking with Moses the Lord refers to the patriarchs in the present tense. Therefore, according to Jesus' logic, they are not dead—but very much alive (Luke 20:20-40).

Not content with this success, Jesus asks who these leaders think the Christ is a descendant of. How can Christ be a descendant of David when David refers to him as Lord? Thus Christ is the Lord of David, not his son. By employing stellar logic Jesus carves the opposition up argumentatively. Jesus uses creative and impressive rational arguments to defeat the moral scientists.

We cannot escape the fact that reason is necessary to advance even the basic thesis of this book. We cannot argue about the nonsense of faith without making some sense to someone or having a starting point by which we all agree on logically. Without logic, all ideas fall apart. This book is nonsense because I use logic to deconstruct logic.

Without reason and logical arguments, what can be said about anything? How do we construct a series of ideas that are built one upon another if we can't rely on logic? Up to this point I have defined the limits of logic in relation to faith. Hopefully, I have created a little more breathing room for faith and restricted the domain of logic to its appropriate place. This does not mean we completely do away with reason and logic; we only want to rid ourselves of the idea of its supremacy.

What this book does endeavor to do is to return reason to its proper place. Reason notices patterns and creates a framework on which to represent ideas. And logic is a gateway through which we can judge the strength of arguments. Especially in the area of how God intersects with the world, reason and logic are able to help us catch echoes of God's work. Through our senses and the reason that springs from our observations, we are able to see these echoes of God in what he is doing in the world. We cannot view the resurrection with our eyes, but we can detect its echo through the record documented in Scripture. We cannot see the creation of the world, but we can hear the echoes of that great event in geology and archaeology. We cannot see God create the trillions of organisms that inhabit the planet, but we can observe this creative event in fossils.

These echoes are not primary things that point to God and the Christian faith. They are second- and third-order indicators that tell us something big happened. As I sit at my office window and watch the construction of a building, I don't need to see every step of the building or witness the workers raising every steel beam to know that it was the product of careful and detailed work of hundreds of skilled workers. The finished building echoes of all the hours of labor that went into its construction.

This is what Thomas Aquinas had in mind when he presented proofs for the existence of God. Aquinas saw God at work in the world and was able to use reason to see what God is doing. Aquinas noticed something simple but profound. He noticed that the planet, the solar system and all the galaxies are in motion. This led him to conclude that something (or someone) had to put them into motion initially. Things don't move on their own. All motion must have a first cause, which Aquinas called a Prime Mover.

Aquinas actually borrows some of these ideas from Aristotle. In his *Metaphysics*, Aristotle concluded that all things in motion were put in motion by something substantial or eternal. Because all things are dependent on other things for their movement, "there is therefore also something which moves it. And since that which is moved and moves is intermediate, there is something which moves without being moved, being eternal, substance and actuality."[2]

Aristotle posits that the Prime Mover must be eternal and actual. God, if you will, is the Prime Mover who set everything in motion. The earth rotates on an axis and orbits the sun. Our galaxy is rotating as well. All this movement was initially generated from something else.

Some might say this motion is the result of a collision of matter billions of years ago, which in turn transferred its explosive energy into everything we see today. Some call it creation, some call it the big bang or the event horizon. The name doesn't rid us of the burden of proof that we face. Whatever we call it, we still have to explain how those elements appeared. Not only that, but why did they have properties that created life? For that matter, where did the idea of properties come from? And we are forced to ask questions like:

1. If primordial elements existed at the beginning of time, why did they explode?

2. If only elements existed and exploded, what was the medium they exploded into?

3. In order for anything to have happened to begin with, it had to have energy to do it with. Where did that energy come from? At one point there had to be an uncaused cause—a prime mover. Where did that come from?

These questions get at the heart of what we are looking for as humans. The origins of things present opportunities to ask and seek answers to why. When we get back to first causes, we are near the creative event and hence the Creator. This is why the evolution and creation debates are charged with passion. They get us close to the intentions of creation and the Creator.

In *Darwin's Black Box: The Biochemical Challenge to Evolution*, Michael Behe discusses the shortfalls of evolutionary theory. Instead of picking on the lack of evidence or the scholarship behind the evolutionary position, Behe centers his argument around the idea of "irreducible complexity."

> By irreducibly complex I mean a single system composed of several well-matched, interacting parts that contribute to the basic function, wherein the removal of any one of the parts causes the system to effectively cease functioning. An

irreducibly complex system cannot be produced directly (that is, by continuously improving the initial function, which continues to work by the same mechanism) by slight, successive modifications of a precursor system, because any precursor to an irreducibly complex system that is missing a part is by definition nonfunctional. An irreducibly complex biological system, if there is such a thing, would be a powerful challenge to Darwinian evolution.[3]

In layman's terms Behe questions how evolution could have produced complex and powerful parts of creatures (e.g., skin and eyeballs) when each stage of mutation offers no specific biological advantage over the rest of the species.

Behe's main illustration that he uses is of a mousetrap. A mousetrap is made up of a system that is irreducibly complex. The components include a platform, spring, hammer, hold-down bar, catch and staples—take any one of these away and the trap fails to work. Behe draws an analogy to evolution by asking what advantage a mousetrap would hold if each component took a generation to evolve. A staple does nothing by itself; neither does the spring or the hammer. Why would evolution go through the successive mutations needed to bring about the components that in themselves add nothing to the organism? Each generation would need a perfect placement of a perfectly formed part that offered absolutely no advantage to the system. The mousetrap only functions when all the pieces are perfectly assembled in their totality. What advantage do biological systems have in partial development?

For example, in the development of the human eye, evolution would argue that billions of years of mutation have developed an organ that can focus and transmit light from the eyeball along the optic nerve into the cerebral cortex to interact with the rest of the human body, which uses stereoscopic vision to locate a baseball in flight and calculates where it will land so that the human can catch it in a baseball glove.

When we examine each stage of that evolutionary journey, it begins to unravel. Since eyeballs don't appear in one generation, our human ancestors must have had successive stages of proto-eyes that developed over eons. During this time lenses, corneas, irises, pupils and foveas must evolve. But for simplicity's sake, let's look at it this way. One generation has no eyes, and then the next generation is born with an eye socket (but no eye). Forgiving the fact that an eye socket is a major change to the face of an animal, what specific advantage does an eye socket present? Let's say the eye socket enables it to survive, and it breeds others with eye sockets and then one other mutation thousands of years later manifests a pre-eyeball liquid sack. Again, liquid sacks provide no functional advantage.

This occurs repeatedly, and the organism goes through thousands of perfectly placed mutations that offer no individual benefit to the organism. Once the eye is fully evolved, it needs another thousand generations of perfectly placed genetic mutations to develop an optic nerve. Once that is fully evolved it needs another ten thousand generations for a fully evolved and perfectly placed cerebral cortex to interpret the optical signals. We begin to see Behe's point.

Most people would probably conclude that over billions of years millions of mutations could produce eyes, hair or a heart, but it is in the assembly of the disparate parts that we begin to appreciate the wonder with which we are made.

Behe challenges evolution within the established rules of evolutionary theory. His question is simple—if systems like the eye or skin or lymph nodes only function and provide a benefit to the organism when fully formed, can the evolutionary step-by-step process accomplish this, even if it has millions of years to do so?

For me, Behe is detecting echoes of God's created order. I am reminded of William Paley's argument in which two men stumble over a watch found along a path in the woods. One looks at it and wonders at the incredible detail and marvels at how it could have assembled itself into such a fine-looking and functional piece of art. The other looks at it and concludes that it is the product of a designer. In fact, the second man concludes that all things with design imply a designer.

Think about that. Design echoes a designer.

Not all echoes are detected by the hard sciences. The records of humans in times past echo throughout history. When we look at the literary record of how God has worked in the world through the course of time, the echoes are unmistakable.

In 1949, near the ancient site of Qumran in Israel, shepherd boys threw a rock into a cave and heard an odd sound. Investigating, the boys found a cave filled with pottery and ancient artifacts. Many of these artifacts turned out to be copies of ancient Hebrew Scriptures that had been preserved over millennia. These and others texts found in nearby caves came to be known as the Dead Sea Scrolls. Prior to the discovery of these scrolls, the oldest manuscripts we had of the Hebrew Bible were separated from the original texts by thousands of years, which allowed for some to speculate that syncretism, embellishment and error had crept into our present-day Old Testament. But the Dead Sea Scrolls brought us much closer to the time when the Old Testament Scriptures were written. When the translating work on the scrolls commenced, everyone was anxious to see how they compared to modern-day Scripture.

Decades later, when the Dead Sea Scrolls were finally published, they revealed that in over in one thousand years of copying the text by hand, the Old Testament text had changed very little. In fact Geza Vermes, noted authority on the Dead Sea Scrolls,

claimed that the experts "are in a position to prove that it has remained virtually unchanged for the last two thousand years."[4]

We hear so much about how the Scriptures of Christianity
have been tainted or added to over the centuries. It is refreshing
to hear an expert in the field claim that the Bible is an accurate
transmission of the original message over thousands of years.
When I hear that the Word of God has been preserved so faith-
fully, I hear echoes of Scripture that claim that "the Word of God
shall stand forever" and "My Word will not return void" (Isaiah
40:8; 55:11).

These echoes are also found in the research of biblical scholar
N. T. Wright. In his book *The Resurrection of the Son of God*,
Wright makes the case that the idea of the resurrection was not a
new idea, but one that had very specific implications for a very
broad audience. The Greeks and Romans believed in the possibility of the ghostly presence of a person after death, but there were
no references to a person being raised corporeally from the dead.
While resurrection circulated among the Jews, it was not universally embraced. Those who did embrace it believed it would happen only at the end of time. Generally, the idea of a person being
raised from the dead was not a possibility (before the last day).

Until about the mid first century A.D.

Apart from the New Testament (a first-century document),
there was no literature that discussed a person dying and rising
physically. The idea of a bodily resurrection was nonsense.

Then, stories of bodily resurrection begin to proliferate—
almost as if a switch was flipped.

> The truly striking thing about all these apparent deaths, and
> their strange reversals or overcomings is how they suddenly
> proliferate in the literature of the middle or late first century
> AD onwards. It would be daring to suggest that this is the

result of the early Christians' story of Jesus making its way in to the wider Greco-Roman world. . . . Equally, it is difficult to give a definite explanation for the famous Greek inscription, from the same period, found near Nazareth: the emperor (unnamed, but almost certainly Claudius) issues an edict warning of penalties for breaking open or violating tombs.[5]

Though as a historian Wright doesn't want to draw specific conclusions about the sudden interest in people rising from the dead in Greek literature, I do. After centuries of no one writing about a physical resurrection from the dead, all of a sudden in Greek literature there is a surge in plot lines dealing with empty tombs. Pretty coincidental.

These echoes of truth call to us across the span of history. How can we not listen to these and be challenged? Perhaps there is a place for reason and logic—but only in the sense that it contributes to the deconstruction of reason as the chief arbiter of truth. When we think of reason and logic as the only vehicle by which we can take hold of truth, we have a problem. But we can use reason to set limits for its own abilities. Reason is powerful when it knows its own function.

13

WHAT CAN I SAY?

I HAVE THIS ANNOYING HABIT that is hard to shake. Whenever I am talking about faith or spiritual things, especially when I am trying to convey a new idea or thought, I keep returning to a particular phrase, asking, "Does that make sense?"

It is annoying because, as we have already explored, when I am talking about faith and spirit, none of it really makes *sense*. It has a logic to it that goes beyond human reason. Even though I know this, out of habit I keep asking people whether it "makes sense." What I really should be asking is, "Am I being clear?" or "Is this something that resonates with you?" As an example, this is a conversation I had a while ago with, Usha, a Hindu friend:

Me: As a Hindu, what do you connect with the most in your religion?

Usha: Well I'm not sure, I have done some pretty bad things in my life, I am still waiting to pay the price for what I have done.

Me: But see, that is the major difference between karma and grace. In karma you get what you deserve. If you have done bad, bad will be done to you. With grace it is completely different. You don't get what you deserve—you get the complete opposite. Grace is the opposite of karma. *Does that make sense?*

Like I said, I should just ask, "Do you know what I mean?" or "What do you think of that?" From an argumentative viewpoint the question of whether it makes any sense is ridiculous. We are talking about the difference between karma and grace, and I am asking if it makes sense. Well of course it doesn't; at least karma is logical—you get what you give! If you give out negative energy, you will receive negative energy. Grace is nothing like that. Grace is completely absurd; you receive what you don't deserve.

Now I know I didn't lose Usha just because I asked her if it made sense, but if we are talking about being okay with the apparently irrational nature of God, we will have to use better terms. We have to rethink the way we talk about faith; otherwise we are still under the burden of logic. For many people, talking about grace invites a lot of questions when we ask, "Does that make sense?" What if the answer is, "Not really. Explain to me again how people like Hitler can receive mercy?" It is no longer important to make sense; the goal is to be clear when talking about a faith system that does not line up with sense and reason.

Consequently, the first thing we should do in talking about a God who works outside the bounds of human reason is point out that God works outside the bounds of human reason. Seems simple, I think, but this is the fight that a lot of Christian publications and speakers engage in. There is a market of Christian thought that tries so hard to emphasize how faith is logical and fits nicely with reason and science. In this book we have looked at the possibility of using the argument of absurdity as a starting point rather than a battleground. So, let's look at the practical ways we can employ this unique way of presenting the truth of faith in our day-to-day conversations.

I was talking with a friend while walking through London, and we happened to stumble on the subject of faith. Ron was obviously a guy who has some objections to traditional faith, and so I thought it would be interesting to see where this would take us. He had mentioned that belief in God is absurd. To which I responded, "I agree. It has to be in order to be true." At first he thought that I agreed with him and continued talking, but then—double take—he returned to my comment and asked me what I meant by it being true. We wound up talking about it for hours.

Now imagine I had engaged him on every point where he had issues with the logic of Christianity. We would have had a spirited conversation but would have gotten nowhere. I have been part of too many conversations that turn into verbal and philosophical Ping-Pong matches. At the end it usually is a draw because there are only the two of us and neither mind has been changed. At best it becomes an exhibition match for different ways of thinking. We pat ourselves on the back because we sounded great, but nothing changes. It can be very frustrating.

Instead, Ron and I started with the conclusion that faith resides outside the limits of reason. This was disorienting to Ron, who had never heard a believer admit so readily that faith is not bound to reason. He had questions, which was wonderful because I spent no time preaching, just trying my best to answer questions about a new way of looking at God. To be honest, it was a subject that continued on for so long that I was surprised that he was interested in it that much. The point is that we were discussing faith, not arguing about its legitimacy.

I have found that it is incredibly difficult to get people interested in talking about faith. Even Christians don't talk about their faith all that much. Typically, pew-sitters don't say much about their faith until someone has objections to it, and then they won't shut up. It is fascinating to me how many quiet Christians become cerebrally engaged when they find someone on whom they can spew all the information they read in their apologetics books. It makes me wonder whether Christianity is composed mainly of people who see faith as an intellectual game to win. We have many arguments about God, but few lead people to him.

Let's be honest, rather than trying to always defend the rationality of the faith, doesn't it just feel right to let others worry about its logic as we simply embrace the Scriptures? But this is where the disconnect occurs—how can someone accept the words of Christ when they are not sure that the human-centered accounts about him are true? This is where our second principle comes into play—we are all on a level playing field when it comes to uncertainty. When we discuss the certainty of the Scriptures I don't emphasize why I think the Bible is an accurate witness. Instead, I note that everything we trust (including the sciences) is uncertain because of the human element in it.

You would have enjoyed seeing Ron's face as we talked about the limits of science. It seemed as if this was the first time he had ever considered the fact that human reason can really only answer the "what" questions and none of the "why" questions. Like someone losing faith in humanity, Ron was perplexed, and we considered the fact that the humanity that recorded the life of Jesus is the same humanity that invented algebra. Mathematics and the sciences did not fall from the heavens. The faith that people put in the sciences is amazing. Consistently remind them that the sciences do not originate outside of the human mind. The assured results of science are just observations of patterns in our world; they are not any closer to the truth of why this world is here or what its purpose is than the Scriptures.

Only a few months ago, as I talked with Nicole, I was fascinated to hear a very intelligent chemistry teacher process the limits of science. When we talked about the fact that seconds, meters, liters and digits are inventions of the human mind, it became clear to her that science suffers from the same problem that it accuses faith of. Our measurements come from the same human-centered sources as our Scriptures do. So science and faith are really on the same level.

Ultimately we want to play up the fact that Christianity is not of the senses, and emphasize agreement with skeptics. Their instincts are usually right. I had a conversation with an older gentleman who was very angry that I was talking about how God is a God of mercy. He had obviously given up on God because that thought seemed too fairy-tale-esque. He pointed to the logic of a system like karma (there's that karma again). "At least karma makes sense; grace is ridiculous," he thundered. He obviously didn't know I was writing a book about this very thing.

Again, instead of arguing the logic of grace, I agreed with him, which startled him. He expected an argument. I think he wanted an argument. Arguments are great ways to hide from the truth. That's why we can't give in to the quest for an argument—there is no argument for God. Instead, I decided to let the bizarre glory of Christ shine in front of us. I looked at the gentleman and I said, "I agree, grace is absurd—who lets someone get away with something and then rewards them?"

He shook his head. (I could tell he was a little nervous about how quickly I agreed with him.) Then I told him, "But you said that it was karma's reasonableness that makes you believe in it; sorry, but I disagree." He looked puzzled and let me continue. "If you place in front of me two systems, karma and grace, you have one that makes sense and the other that doesn't, correct?" He nodded his head, slightly annoyed and wanting to continue his rant. "Now think about it. If one makes sense and the other doesn't, and you are asking me which comes from a divine source, we would have to rule out the one that makes sense just because of the suspicion that it could have easily come from a human mind."

He wasn't sure, so I continued, "If you have karma that is reasonable and grace that is not, which one do you think is most likely the product of a human mind?" He thought for a second and then answered, "Karma." "Me too!" I responded. "In fact, I think the truth that grace is absurd helps nail down its divine source. So if you are asking me to guess which side we should sign up for, which side we should align ourselves with, it is the side that gives me the crazy stuff, the things that have origins outside human logic."

Well, he didn't budge much because we know that people aren't argued into the kingdom of God. At this point the man would need to encounter the person of Christ in the gracious actions of Christ's followers, which brings me to my next point. We don't have arguments for God, because God didn't either. Remember, God didn't send us a list of ideas, hoping we'd catch on. God sent us a series of laws that were completed in the person of Jesus. God didn't just argue with us, he let his ideas come to life in the way he approached the human race. We should do the same.

The way that we behave, the way that we move through the world, is the most winsome way to convince people of their need for Christ. The agreement that faith is nonsense disarms people and moves us past the point of disagreement. Once they agree that faith is not in the realm of logic, they can take note of our lives, which are (or should be) in rhythm with God's purposes.

So if there is no argument for God, how do we argue? Well, for starters, we don't have to argue anything. In fact, the minute we involve our puny minds in the search for truth, we have to remember that we are automatically distorting it by processing it through our brains. Even faith can be distorted in our effort to quantify, objectify, analyze and flatten it. So stop arguing.

The first step in the process of talking with people about faith is to quickly come to the point of agreement. Christians are stereotyped as being close-minded and backward. Because we don't readily accept "facts," many see us as having our heads buried in the sand. To counter this perception, show them very quickly that you agree: "Yes, Christianity is a strain on logic." Don't be surprised if they wait for the sucker punch. The people I talk with search my face for the other shoe to drop and are worried that they have been manipulated into some sort of Socratic argument. I very quickly alleviate their fears and say, "No, you are right. How can the Christian faith make sense?" It is pure nonsense: a Son of God, a dying and rising Messiah, the concept of grace—all of it is crazy, and strains logic most of the time.

If I am cultivating a friendship, I usually let these ideas soak in for a while. It might be days or months before I usually get the question "How can you believe in something that is so absurd?" This leads to step two: helping people remember that we are all on the same footing. I usually begin by pointing out that everything that we put our trust in is a human construct. If the person I am talking with is an agnostic, it's probably because no one has ever demonstrated that people ought to put their faith in something beyond what they can see and prove and verify. I ask gentle questions like "What are the rock-sure things you put your faith in?"

"I believe in what I can see and prove."

"Like what?"

"Like, I am here, and this walkway supports my weight, and food will give me energy, and my family gives me love and support—those things that I can see and touch and taste and feel—things that are real. If I am sick, I take antibiotics, and they fight the infection, which has been shown to be true. Prayer is a nice idea, but that is all it is."

And so I agree with most of what he says—these are things we grasp with our senses and call real. But then I start to chip away at the confidence we have in these things. Is it really true that because I happen to know how the world works (like walkways give support, friends and family are loving, and antibiotics fight bacterial infection) that these things alone are real? In other words, just because we have figured out how to manipulate the world around us to get what we want (predictability, love and health), does this mean that we know there is nothing beyond these things that could be true as well? All we have done is figured out how to manipulate the environment around us to deliver the things that we need or want. We are no closer to getting at what is real than when we started.

For example: I get an infection and take an antibiotic. Just because I have figured out that an antibiotic helps me feel better has not gotten me any closer to what is ultimately real than discovering that food gets rid of hunger or breathing helps me live longer. Doing these things (taking medicine, eating good meals, breathing) might be a great way to thrive in this world, but this does not mean I have discovered what is real about the world. What made me need air? How did I come to inhabit this body with lungs, blood cells and an intricate cardiopulmonary system? Now *that* would be knowing what is real. All reason can do is tell us how things work—not why they work that way.

In fact, there are a lot of things that we think we know but we don't. Newton "discovered" gravity, but what did he really do? He noticed an effect in our world and came up with some pretty amazing ideas on its properties. He was no closer to what is real than you or I. Einstein built on Newton and developed the idea that massive objects like the Earth put a wrinkle in space-time and cause things near them to be drawn into the warp that they create. Great ideas, wonderful reasoning, but it only describes something to us. We are still at a loss as to why. In fact, the arrival at this discovery becomes arbitrary when we think about it. So we know what gravity is, but we are still ignorant about why it is. The sciences are built on the back of a network of human ideas (numbers, measurements, and values like "hot" and "cold") that are completely arbitrary in this universe. Though we have done an amazing job at showing the patterns built into our world, the sciences have done a poor job at unmasking the purpose of it all.

So in effect, we are both on the same level. The human-centered sources of revelation are also the human-centered sources of scientific calculations. The sciences are human constructs just as much as religion. Then I usually get the question, "So what makes you put your trust in religion, if science and faith are on the same level? At least we can observe the sciences."

Notice how at this point my friend is asking for my input, so I don't have to feel the pressure to argue or theorize or convince. I simply reply that it is the uncanny *oddness* of faith that attracts me to Jesus. When I think through all the sciences, I love the fact that they make sense and lead me to greater knowledge. I love reading about astronomy and how galaxies are whirling away from us at breakneck speed. The shift on the light spectrum reveals whether they are moving toward or away from us. I love the precision of it and how it all fits together. But this precisely reveals the ceiling of knowledge and the intrusion of the rational mind. Just as an athe-ist might say that it is human nature to look for gods, the sciences—which are no different—look for patterns. We observe patterns because we look for patterns.

However, when I see things that break patterns and are absurd, I take notice. This is the last stage of my apologetic. The absurd bears the signature of something beyond the human mind. In fact, redaction criticism—a branch of literary scholarship that at-tempts to discover how an editor (redactor) shaped a biblical narrative—states that the sayings attributed to Jesus that pose the most theological problems are probably the most true. No one "cleaned them up" so they would fit the established canon. Their glaring "otherness" is a witness to their authenticity.

In the same way, when I consider faith, I look for the system that is way "out there," which strikes me as having come from a mind outside of humanity. And I don't mean that I follow Egyptian mythology (with its crazy stories of a primordial tongue oozing out from the sea). I don't believe in Greek mythology that has Zeus cavorting with everything that moves. I am not a fan of the Eastern religions that detail Lakshmi and Sita's escapades with the Monkey People. I am not talking about the epic stories of ancient America or Africa. Grandiosity does not make the most compelling story. (And there are plenty of fantastic stories bandied about.)

What moves me is the counterintuitiveness of the idea. When I compare the major religions, every one of which prescribes a way to God, I begin to see a similarity that is rooted in the human attempt to find something beyond. But Christianity describes the opposite—namely, though God is unapproachable, God seeks us—a completely different concept. We read about this as far back as Genesis, in which God makes covenants with humans. He even seals one covenant with Abraham (Genesis 15) by putting his own life on the line. The continuity of this principle is evidenced thousands of years later in the life of Jesus. The Son of God comes to Earth. He is called Immanuel or "God among us." He again puts his life on the line on our behalf. There is something radically different in all of this.

And this difference is found not just in the larger picture of God and how he behaves, but in the way that Jesus calls us to live in rhythm with a God who acts contrary to the prevailing human ethic of self-preservation and survival. There is something so extravagantly foreign about every facet of the Christian faith that makes me wonder where it was all cooked up. Some people look at religion as being invented by people who long for an eternal daddy or a sense of eternal justice. Perhaps Christianity deserves a second look, when you consider how Jesus' appeal is for us to die to self.

Finally, if we believe that Christ is alive and well today, we need to present him as our last step in communicating about God. We have no argument, but we know the person of Christ. We can lead people through these steps that call for a reappraisal of the human-centered approach to what is true, but it all culminates in their own will. They have to come to a point where they are willing to address the person of Christ. They have to be willing to take all of this two-dimensional thought and flat conversation, and meet the three-dimensional Jesus. We can encourage this movement toward Christ verbally, but it needs to be echoed in the way we walk through this world. If we move through the world with a different cadence, one in rhythm with God, it can help move our friends to want to encounter the person of Christ for themselves.

So whereas a lot rides on the fact that there is no argument for God, it still can't beat the most persuasive truth that a person can encounter: the three-dimensional presence of Christ in you. You can have all the conversation in the world about the depth of a relationship with God, but if it is not observed in your life, then both of you are misled.

14

THE DREAM OF GOD

CERTAIN MOMENTS IN EVERYONE'S LIFE are reserved for dreaming or zoning out. I love these moments. They are magical. It's like the whole universe stands still or I am transported to another dimension. It happens when I'm sitting on a beach looking at the ocean. The consistency of the surf and the gleam of the moon over the waves can put me in a Zen-like state. Watching a fire does the same. I have seen everyone from grown men to little children be mesmerized by the flames. Gazing at the stars is another such moment. Sitting back and staring at the vast expanse of the universe is intoxicating. Usually at times like this the deeper questions come out: *Are we alone in the universe? Is there life out there?*

At times like these my inner child appears. I feel vulnerable and small. It reminds me of the movie *Contact*, starring Jodie Foster. A little girl is looking through a telescope at stars as the night settles in. She looks up at her father and asks whether he thinks there is any intelligent life out there. Her father weighs his answer thoughtfully: "I guess I'd say if it is just us . . . seems like an awful waste of space."

This sentiment is probably shared by most people. I mean, think of it—there are billions of stars in the universe, each star system with the possibility of a planet that sustains life. It would seem arrogant to assume that the only life in the universe is on planet Earth. Why indeed would God create this big universe if it is only meant for us?

Astronomer Frank Drake, now president of the Search for Extra-Terrestrial Intelligence (SETI) program, developed an equation to determine whether there was life out there. The equation has a series of factors: the rate of star formation per year in our galaxy, the fraction of those stars that have planets, the average number that can support planets and so on. The equation looks like this: $N = R^\star \times fp \times ne \times f\,e \times fi \times fc \times L$.[1]

I am no mathematician. When I look at these letters I have no idea what they mean, but it looks impressive. When the right numbers were plugged into the formula, the result was (drum roll please) that there are an estimated ten planets within our galaxy.

Are you serious? Only ten? In fact, as science continues to refine its understanding of the universe, a more recent computation of this value led to an estimation of two. Two planets in our galaxy?

Now I realize that the Drake equation is debated back and forth, and there have been many scientists who have come up with different values, but ten planets is pretty anticlimactic. I want my money back. That has to be the most depressing figure for people searching for extraterrestrials. Talk about finding a needle in a haystack. As we have refined our capabilities, the search for extraterrestrial life has led us to expect a smaller, not greater, possibility of life elsewhere in the universe.

So perhaps it is arrogant to wonder whether we may be the only ones here on earth, but then again it may be backed up by good science. Maybe the vast universe is a waste of space. It is natural to think that the universe would have to have life somewhere else because there is life on earth. We can't be the exception to what is happening in the universe, can we? Maybe. But what if we look at the night sky and don't see wasted space, but rather an empty room . . .

An empty room?

Yes, an empty room. Maybe that space is meant for us. When we ponder the night sky, instead of assuming that we are some random blip among many random blips, we should view it from the perspective that we are the purpose of creation. The idea of our own insignificance is a relatively new development in the history of human thought. Maybe we were right to begin with. Perhaps all of this space around us is an enormous room waiting to be used, an endless potential lying dormant.

When God created the world, it was all very good. The refrain "and God saw that it was good" appears repeatedly in Genesis 1. Good for what? For its own sake! Whatever God creates is by its own right good. If God is good, whatever God does is good. But now think about the step-by-step manner in which he created. At first things are formless and void and then God creates light, land, seas, plants and animals—each stage providing for the next created thing to prosper. All of it good.

And humans are the crowning achievement of God's creation. This statement is not arrogant for two reasons. First, it is not our achievement but God's. God did something extraordinarily good, and we are the result. We were blobs of clay. Our role in the process was passive; God gets all the credit. Second, creation's week did not end with humans. The pinnacle of the creation week is the seventh day, when God took a break and enjoyed what he created. Humanity was one of several elements that contributed to God's enjoyment of creation. We are not the purpose of creation—God's enjoyment is. We are God's work—something he was delighted to create and enjoy. This helps us have a proper assessment of who we are as created beings.

Everything God had created was perfect—without sin or fault. No disease, no decay, no taxes, no death. All that Adam and Eve knew in the Garden of Eden was goodness and life. Imagine that—no death. Everything changes when there is no death. Death brings fear, pain, decay and uncertainty, but perhaps the biggest change it introduces is the concept of time. Without death, there are an infinite number of minutes, days and years. A day on a scale of trillions of years is almost meaningless. Time only exists when there is something like death to put a cap on life. Because of death, each moment of life has special value.

Life without death also changes the space we inhabit. Imagine no hospitals, cemeteries, nursing homes, funeral parlors. But if no one died, we would quickly outgrow this planet. According to the Population Reference Bureau, 106 billion people have been born since the beginning of humanity.[2] This estimate is specious. How do we really begin to estimate who was alive thousands of years ago? But we need a number to start with, and this is as good as any. Our current population in the world is over six billion people. Imagine more than seventeen times the present world population inhabiting the planet.

Now couple a zero-death rate with an infinite amount (for lack of a better word) of time. We would need more room! So, what if that was part of the plan? If you have an infinite amount of time and the mandate to multiply (Genesis 1:22), doesn't an ever-expanding universe make sense? The universe seems like a pretty suitable home for the unlimited growth of the human race. Is it possible that this is the original dream of God? The universe could very well have been the home that God built for a never-ending and increasingly multiplying race of humans and creatures.

But how would we get there? Imagine what it would be like for humans to have a relationship with their Creator that is not adversarial. No barrier, no shame, no loss—friendship with God is the norm. What would limit the human imagination? What hurdles would there be for the friends of God? Prayers are face-to-face conversations, hopes are realized, and dreams have an ally in the Creator of the universe. What would stop human progress?

In this world without sin, cities are amazing, cars don't pollute, no one is hungry or in want. Houses are fantastic—some big, some small, all of them products of healthy wishes and desires. Each person has a job, varied in earnings, without a hint of jealousy, bitterness or envy. When mishaps occur (broken bones, cuts, bruises) God is their healer. Someone undoubtedly would come up with the idea of exploring the heavens. Perhaps God would help, but I wonder if he would let us figure it out on our own. I believe it's God's dream that we fly, float or beam up to parts of the universe and use up all that "wasted" space. The room that God built for us—ever expanding, never-ending.

Now, however, we see it as nothing but loss.

God's dream was interrupted by rebellious humans, and death entered creation. Life is stunted by disease and death. God's dream became a nightmare of death and decay. Now, when we look up at the sky, we see wasted space. A waste of potential.

We are now doomed to nothing but our minds—what we think, feel and know. God's will is foreign to us. It's like learning another language—we are capable of learning it, but it's not our mother tongue. So here we are in this huge expanse, an incredible architectural wonder—wasted space.

And yet this is just the interval between two luminous times. Part of our sense of disconnectedness comes from existing within the physical framework of the dream of God but knowing that there is something more that was intended. That gnawing we feel looking up at the sky is a symptom of the malaise of sin—we were meant for more than this. The fact that the universe echoes the dream of God, one day to be realized but currently interrupted, is both depressing and intriguing.

This place that we find ourselves in—wasted space—waits for the dream of God to intersect it. But something has to happen first. We must realize that the loss goes beyond the spatial. It extends to our ability to think outside of our heads.

Examining scientific thought from the realm of the dream is depressing. We mistakenly believe that only what is before us is real; there is nothing more to life than what we bring to it. Think of that—I don't know whether it is more arrogant or depressing. We had no say in our being here. No one willed him- or herself into existence, and yet many believe that the only possible explanation for the universe, for life, comes solely through our senses. How sad to arrive at the conclusion that I am undoubtedly here yet God isn't. It is miraculous that I exist—but God can't exist. We rarely examine this way of thinking from the outside. How sad.

But this is precisely what we are left with when we are limited to our own minds. Revelation always trumps empirical data because the senses tell us only what we can see while revelation tells us what we can't. We can see only from our very limited place within the universe. We need a view from the perspective of the One who created the universe—not only what his intentions were in the first place but beyond the brief span of sin.

Thankfully it is not the end of the story. God has a plan to reopen the heavens to reveal his original intention for the world. Wouldn't it be nice? Well, yes, it would—and it is. There is substance behind our hopes, and it comes in the form of revelation. We can't discover God's plans for the future by examining the shards of glass on the floor. We need to answer the door.

The idea begins in the Old Testament. In Ezekiel God says:

I will make a covenant of peace with them; it will be an

everlasting covenant. I will establish them and increase their numbers, and I will put my sanctuary among them forever. My dwelling place will be with them; I will be their God, and they will be my people. Then the nations will know that I the LORD make Israel holy, when my sanctuary is among them forever. (Ezekiel 37:26-28)

In the future God and humans are again united—as we were in the Garden of Eden. Wouldn't it be nice? Yes, and *good!* God makes an everlasting covenant with us and places his sanctuary—his house—with us. And we become his people. Then God accomplishes what he intended in the first place.

Jeremiah has a similar vision of God's dream of the future, but he provides more detail. God will write his law not on stone but on our hearts, and we will be changed by his tangible presence.

"This is the covenant I will make with the house of Israel
    after that time," declares the LORD.
"I will put my law in their minds
    and write it on their hearts.
I will be their God,
    and they will be my people.

"No longer will a man teach his neighbor,
    or a man his brother, saying, 'Know the LORD,'
because they will all know me,
    from the least of them to the greatest,"
        declares the LORD.
"For I will forgive their wickedness
    and will remember their sins no more."
(Jeremiah 31:33-34)

Our relationship with God will be so intimate the Old Testament portrays it as a marriage. Isaiah 54:5 states that "your Maker is your husband," and the entire book of Hosea is a marriage parable between God and humans. In the New Testament the church is called the bride of Christ (2 Corinthians 11:2; Revelation 19:7; 21:2, 9; 22:17).

In John 14, Jesus speaks of leaving the disciples but quickly assures them that he is working on something that will bring about great good.

> Do not let your hearts be troubled. Trust in God; trust also in me. In my Father's house are many rooms; if it were not so, I would have told you. I am going there to prepare a place for you. And if I go and prepare a place for you, I will come back and take you to be with me that you also may be where I am. (John 14:1-3)

It seems that the disciples would have understood this as marriage language. After the betrothal, a young man would return to his father's house to build a wedding suite where the newlyweds would consummate the marriage. As the room was nearing completion the young man would look to his father for approval that his work was complete. When asked if the wedding was soon, the incipient groom would respond, "Only my father knows." The bride-to-be would have a lamp at the ready in case her future husband arrived unexpectedly. It's remarkable that Jesus told his disciples that he was preparing a place for them (and us as well). When people asked him about his return, he said only the Father knows (Matthew 24:36).

Revelation closes the dramatic sweep of Scripture with the arrival of Christ and the ensuing wedding feast:

> Then I heard what sounded like a great multitude, like the roar of rushing waters and like loud peals of thunder, shouting:

"Hallelujah!
For our Lord God Almighty reigns.
Let us rejoice and be glad
and give him glory!
For the wedding of the Lamb has come,
and his bride has made herself ready.
Fine linen, bright and clean,
was given her to wear."
(Fine linen stands for the righteous acts of the saints.)

Then the angel said to me, "Write: 'Blessed are those who are invited to the wedding supper of the Lamb!'" And he added, "These are the true words of God." (Revelation 19:6-9)

It's God's dream that Jesus will return to claim his bride, the church—those who believe in Christ and live according to the kingdom of God. When that day comes, God will realize his dream—the dwelling place of God and humans will be the same:

Then I saw a new heaven and a new earth, for the first heaven and the first earth had passed away, and there was no longer any sea. I saw the Holy City, the new Jerusalem, coming down out of heaven from God, prepared as a bride beautifully dressed for her husband. And I heard a loud voice from the throne saying, "Now the dwelling of God is with men, and he will live with them. They will be his people, and God himself will be with them and be their God. He will wipe every tear from their eyes. There will be no more death or mourning or crying or pain, for the old order of things has passed away."

He who was seated on the throne said, "I am making everything new!" Then he said, "Write this down, for these words are trustworthy and true." (Revelation 21:1-5)

Isn't that nice?

ACKNOWLEDGMENTS

I wish to acknowledge John Netzel, Dan Simon, Paul Slimmon and Larry Burd for a second chance.

To Walt Mueller, Chap Clark, Kenda Dean and Tony Campolo for their extra push.

To Jason Mitchell and Mike Clauser for their help with editing and teaching me at life.

To David Ashcraft and John Zeswitz for the opportunities given to me.

To Brian Schaub, Jim Deck, Ryan Geeseman, Nate Hamilton, Kelly Seaman, Julie Andreatti for all their help with the art, website and support. It was really cool to have others looking out for you.

To Mom—thanks for the big words.

To Dad—thanks for encouraging me to raise my hand.

To Sue, Charles and Jim for the funny stories and the long debates at dinnertime.

To Tyler, Aedan and Kylie for keeping me young (let's go hiking).

And a great big acknowledgment to my lovely wife, Nikki, who keeps it all together—like a fine wine you get better with age. I'm the lucky one.

NOTES

Chapter 1: Wouldn't It Be Nice?
[1]C. S. Lewis, *Mere Christianity* (New York: HarperSanFrancisco, 1980), p. 39.

Chapter 2: Seeing Things for the First Time
[1]Rodney Clapp, *A Peculiar People: The Church as Culture in a Post-Christian Society* (Downers Grove, Ill.: InterVarsity Press, 1996), p. 98.

Chapter 3: Stop Making Sense
[1]William James, *Pragmatism* (1907; reprint, Cambridge, Mass.: Harvard University Press, 1979), p. 104.

[2]Protagoras, DK 80B1, *Die Fragmente der Vorsocratiker,* ed. H. Diels and W. Kranz (Berlin: Weidmannsche Verlagsbuchhandlung, 1960).

[3]Richard H. Popkin, *The History of Skepticism from Savonarola to Bayle* (New York: Oxford University Press, 2003), p. 41.

[4]Ibid.

[5]John C. Whitcomb and Henry M. Morris, *The Genesis Flood: The Biblical Record and Its Scientific Implications* (Phillipsburg, N.J.: Presbyterian and Reformed, 1961).

[6]Ray Bradbury, *Stories: 100 of His Most Celebrated Tales* (New York: HarperCollins, 2003), p. 264.

Chapter 4: Two-Dimensional Existence
[1]Jürgen Habermas, *Knowledge and Human Interests,* trans. Jeremy Shapiro (Boston: Beacon, 1971), p. 9.

[2]"The Honey Bee Dance Language," North Carolina State University Research <www.cals.ncsu.edu/entomology/apiculture/PDF%20files/1.11.pdf>.

[3]Bertrand Russell, *Science and Reason* (New York: Oxford University Press, 1997), p. 243.

[4]For more development on this topic, consider reading Immanuel Kant, *Critique of Pure Reason,* trans. and ed. Paul Guyer and Allen Wood (Cambridge, Mass.: Cambridge University Press, 1997).

[5]Aristotle *Metaphysics* 1.1.10.

[6]Immanuel Kant, *Kant's Critiques,* ed. Marcus Weigelt (London: Penguin, 2008), p. 48.

Chapter 5: All in Your Head

[1]Richard Dawkins, *The God Delusion* (Boston: Houghton Mifflin, 2006), p. 173.

[2]Robert Audi, *Epistemology: A Contemporary Introduction to the Theory of Knowledge* (London: Routledge, 1998), p. 132.

[3]Ludwig Wittgenstein, *Tractatus Logico-Philosophicus,* trans. D. F. Pears and B. F. McGuinness (New York: Humanities Press, 1961), p. 105.

[4]Philip Clayton, *God and Contemporary Science* (Grand Rapids: Eerdmans, 1997), p. 99.

Chapter 7: In the Flesh

[1]Thomas Cahill, *The Gifts of the Jews: How a Tribe of Desert Nomads Changed the Way Everyone Thinks and Feels* (New York: Doubleday, 1998), p. 108.

[2]William Herzog, *Jesus, Justice and the Reign of God: A Ministry of Liberation* (Louisville: Westminster Press, 2000), p. 169.

[3]H. H. Ben-Sasson, ed., *History of the Jewish People* (Cambridge, Mass.: Harvard University Press, 1976), p. 163.

[4]Cahill, *Gifts of the Jews,* p. 156.

[5]William Barclay, *The Gospel of John* (Edinburgh: St. Andrews Press, 2001), pp. 141-42.

Chapter 8: No Stranger to Nonsense

[1]William Barrett, *Irrational Man: A Study in Existential Philosophy* (Garden City, N.Y.: Doubleday, 1958).

[2]Eric Voegelin, *Order and History,* vol. 2, *The World of the Polis* (Columbia: University of Missouri Press, 2000), p. 305.

[3]Peter M. Phillips, *The Prologue of the Fourth Gospel* (London: T & T Clark, 2006), p. 94.

[4]Plato, *The Last Days of Socrates,* trans. Hugh Tredennick (Harmondsworth, U.K.: Penguin, 1993), pp. 65, 79, 82.

Chapter 9: Circular Reasoning

[1]Michel de Montaigne, "The Apology for Raymond Sebond," in *Skepticism: An Anthology,* ed. Richard Henry Popkin and José Raimundo Maia Neto (New York: Prometheus, 2007), p. 103.

[2]Taken from an interview with Dr. Tony Campolo, October 18, 2010, at Eastern University, St. Davids, Pennsylvania.

[3]Carl Sagan, *The Demon-Haunted World: Science as a Candle in the Dark* (New

York: Ballantine, 1996), p. 295.

[4]Ibid., p. 35.

[5]See, for example, Dr. Arroway's comments in Carl Sagan, *Contact* (New York: Pocket Books, 1985).

[6]Albert Einstein, quoted in James Haught, *2000 Years of Disbelief* (Amherst, N.Y.: Prometheus, 1996).

[7]James Haught, ed., *The Portable Nietzsche* (New York: Viking, 1954), p. 635.

[8]Friedrich Nietzsche, *Thus Spoke Zarathustra,* trans. Clancy Martin (New York: Barnes and Noble Classics, 2005), p. 75.

[9]Mark Twain, *Notebooks,* p. 198, quoted in Nicole Amare and Alan Manning, "Lynching Mark Twain, the Prophet," in *The Mark Twain Annual* 3 (2006): 108.

[10]Christopher Hitchens, *The Portable Atheist: Essential Readings for the Non-believer* (Philadelphia: Da Capo, 2007), p. 480.

[11]Daniel Dennett, *Darwin's Dangerous Idea* (New York: Simon & Schuster, 1995), p. 18.

Chapter 10: Dialogue

[1]Thomas Cahill, *The Gifts of the Jews* (New York: Random House, 1999), especially the great treatment of early citizens of Ur (pp. 43-50, 56-64). Much of this chapter is inspired by Cahill's imaginative storytelling.

[2]See Millard Erickson, *The Word Became Flesh* (Grand Rapids: Baker Academic, 1996), p. 126.

Chapter 12: Echoes of God

[1]Francis Brown, S. R. Driver and Charles A. Briggs, *The Brown-Driver-Briggs Hebrew and English Lexicon* (Peabody, Mass.: Hendrickson, 2005), p. 406.

[2]Aristotle, *Introduction to Aristotle,* ed. Richard McKeon (New York: Random House, 1947), p. 284.

[3]Michael Behe, *Darwin's Black Box: The Biochemical Challenge to Evolution* (New York: Free Press, 2006), p. 39.

[4]Geza Vermes, *The Dead Sea Scrolls in English* (London: Penguin Books, 1987), p. xiv.

[5]N. T. Wright, *The Resurrection of the Son of God* (Minneapolis: Fortress Press, 2003), p. 75.

Chapter 14: The Dream of God

[1]"Drake Equation," *SETI Institute,* 2010 <www.seti.org/drakeequation>.

[2]Carl Haub, "How Many People Have Ever Lived on Earth?" *Population Reference Bureau,* February 1995 <www.prb.org/Articles/2002/HowManyPeople HaveEverLivedonEarth.aspx>.

ABOUT THE AUTHOR

After completing his undergraduate studies at Penn State University, a Master of Divinity degree from Gordon-Conwell Theological Seminary and a doctorate in Youth and Family Ministry at Fuller Theological Seminary, John Wilkinson entered into vocational ministry, ultimately arriving at LCBC Church in Pennsylvania, where he lives with his wife, Nikki. At LCBC he is developing a culture of ministry that fosters meaningful connections between teens and adults and engages senior high students into the adult church community.

John knows a few languages and has the most varied library of anyone on staff. On his time off he enjoys puttering around in his garage workshop, taking bike rides with his family and learning the newest technological gadget on the market.

If you'd like to interact with John about *No Argument for God* or read more of his observations about faith and reason, visit his website at

www.noargumentforgod.com